NEW DIRECTIONS FOR PROGRAM EVALUATION
A Publication of the American Evaluation Association

Nick L. Smith, *Syracuse University*
*EDITOR-IN-CHIEF*

# Evaluation and Social Justice: Issues in Public Education

Kenneth A. Sirotnik
*University of Washington*

*EDITOR*

Number 45, Spring 1990

JOSSEY-BASS INC., PUBLISHERS
San Francisco • Oxford

Evaluation and Social Justice: Issues in Public Education.
*Kenneth A. Sirotnik* (ed.).
New Directions for Program Evaluation, no. 45.

NEW DIRECTIONS FOR PROGRAM EVALUATION
*Nick L. Smith,* Editor-in-Chief

NEW DIRECTIONS FOR PROGRAM EVALUATION is part of The Jossey-Bass
Higher Education and Social and Behavioral Science Series and is
published quarterly by Jossey-Bass Inc., Publishers (publication
number USPS 449-050).

EDITORIAL CORRESPONDENCE should be sent to the Editor-in-Chief,
Nick L. Smith, School of Education, Syracuse University,
330 Huntington Hall, Syracuse, New York 13244-2340.

Library of Congress Catalog Card Number LC 85-644749

International Standard Serial Number ISSN 0164-7989

International Standard Book Number ISBN 1-55542-834-7

Manufactured in the United States of America. Printed on acid-free paper.

*Michael Q. Patton,* Minnesota Extension Service,
University of Minnesota
*Mark St. John,* Inverness Research Associates, Inverness, California
*Thomas A. Schwandt,* Educational Psychology,
Northern Illinois University
*Lee B. Sechrest,* Psychology, University of Arizona
*William R. Shadish, Jr.,* Psychology, Memphis State University
*John K. Smith,* Education, University of Northern Iowa
*Charles B. Stalford,* OERI, Washington, D.C.
*Carol H. Weiss,* Education, Harvard University

AMERICAN EVALUATION ASSOCIATION, 9555 PERSIMMON TREE ROAD, POTOMAC, MD 20854

# CONTENTS

# Editor's Notes

Where are the values in evaluation? Are they to be extracted from the empirical world through the objective application of modern day evaluation technology? Perhaps they can be to some extent. But is not evaluation a fundamentally moral enterprise? Are not choices regarding epistemological and methodological issues in evaluation rooted in fundamental values, beliefs, and human interests? If evaluation of social programs is to serve the interests of society, then should not techniques and procedures derive from, rather than frame, the moral and ethical dimensions of the evaluative problem?

In this volume, we explore the implications of answering these questions in the affirmative. Moreover, the implications are explored relative to a moral and ethical stance rooted in conceptions of social justice. The issues we raise and attempt to deal with are complex and controversial, and closure will not be forthcoming. What is most important, however, is furthering the ongoing dialectic between serving the interests of individuals and serving the interests of society.

Our arguments are especially relevant to public education and the purpose of the public school: to provide equal *and* excellent education for all children in a democratic society. It could be argued, however, that the basic issues to be explored are generic, and parallel discussions could be constructed for the various human sciences, such as social welfare, criminal justice, health services, urban planning, and so forth. However, addressing just one area—public education—is challenge enough. The purpose of this volume is to introduce and discuss the basic issues in order to promote further dialogue.

Given the profound nature of the issue we are considering, four broad topic areas have been delineated so the issue of evaluation and social justice can be conceptualized and analyzed in philosophical and methodological terms. First, it is necessary to develop working concepts of social justice in both philosophical and educational forms so that implications for the theory and practice of evaluation can be determined. Second, these implications must be explicated in a way that makes clear the intimate connection between an ethical stance rooted in social justice and a methodological stance rooted in the socio-political context of evaluation. Third, at least one evaluative model should be explored as a way of synthesizing a commitment to an underlying conception of social justice and to improving educational practice at the school level. Fourth, the foregoing concepts should be further discussed in a programmatic context that lends itself to exploring the dilemmas of the ethics, politics, and methods of evaluation.

## Overview of the Chapters

The four chapters of this volume reflect the rationale outlined above. In Chapter One, David P. Ericson argues that the practice of evaluation and educational evaluators themselves are inescapably confronted with the classic issue of distributive social justice. He then goes on to examine the issue of evaluation and social justice in relation to the distributive behavior of the educational system—that is, the distribution of various benefits (such as knowledge and skills) and opportunities (such as access to further schooling or to special educational programs). He argues that the educational system generally distributes its benefits on the meritocratic grounds of ability, tenacity, and choice, while the social/economic system distributes benefits largely on the basis of the distribution of educational benefits. In other words, the implicit conception of social justice in our society is educationally based and meritocratic. Ericson concludes by arguing that this view may be morally unacceptable and that, at minimum, present evaluation practice requires reevaluation and change to meet the requirements of more adequate standards of social justice.

Ernest R. House, in Chapter Two, examines the ways in which the methodology of evaluation is connected to theories and conceptions of social justice. He argues that theories of justice are historically contingent on current political structures and that the methods employed to evaluate social programs reflect these particular conceptions of justice. House critically examines actual evaluations and specific evaluation methodologies to illustrate how these research procedures work in practice to sustain the theories of justice they reflect. He concludes by suggesting ways to make our research procedures more democratic.

Adopting an essentially egalitarian position on social justice as described in Chapter One and advocated in Chapter Two, Jeannie Oakes and I suggest an evaluation paradigm consistent with this normative stance. The paradigm—critical inquiry—is at once empirical, explanatory, interpretive, deliberative, reflective, instrumental, and action oriented. But it is also critical in the sense that it includes rigorous methods for challenging underlying human interests and ideology, based on explicit commitments to the ideals of justice as fairness. This chapter explores the principles underlying what it means to reconceptualize evaluation as critical inquiry as well as the application of these principles in the context of public schooling.

Finally, in Chapter Four, Virginia Richardson provides a case in point for the themes developed in the preceding chapters on the relationship between evaluation and social justice. However, she begins the normative grounding for her argument in an ethic of caring and goes on to develop the implications of this ethic for the fair and equitable treatment of all children. The substantive context for her discussion is the current wave of programs for the so-called at-risk student. Based on conceptual argument and empirical study, Richardson provides cogent examples of how different theories and definitions of *at-risk* reflect different conceptions of social justice and of how children ought to be cared for in schools. Holding a caring relationship between the teacher and the taught paramount, she argues for evaluation paradigms that explicitly challenge educational practices in terms of whether or not they are serving the best interests of all students.

The idea for an issue on evaluation and social justice originated out of a deep concern about the questions and dilemmas arising from the social roles and functions of program evaluation. Professor Jonathan Z. Shapiro of the College of Education, Louisiana State University, first proposed this project. I and the other contributors to the present volume deeply regret his untimely death, and we extend our sympathies to his friends and loved ones.

It is our sincere hope that the present volume does justice to the vision that Dr. Shapiro may have had in mind. We have tried to provide a context for the seriousness of the issues and some beginning heuristics for confronting the normative content of evaluation theory and practice. We hope we have stimulated further inquiry into the problems and prospects for considerations of social justice in designing and conducting evaluations in social settings.

Kenneth A. Sirotnik
Editor

*Kenneth A. Sirotnik is professor and chair of Policy, Governance, and Administration, College of Education, University of Washington. His work and publications range widely over many topics, including measurement, statistics, evaluation, computer technology, educational policy, organizational change, and school improvement.*

*The reluctance of the evaluation community to confront
issues of social justice in the educational system reflects a
misunderstanding of the appropriate nature of value analysis
in evaluation and the paramount role of social justice concerns
in evaluating social programs and institutions.*

# Social Justice, Evaluation,
# and the Educational System

*David P. Ericson*

The strong revival of normative moral and political theory in the past
few decades opens up fresh possibilities for rethinking the aim and task
of evaluation practices. Whereas the political philosopher T. D. Weldon
pronounced, at the midpoint of this century, that political theory was
dead and buried—the clear victim of a voracious philosophy of science
known variously as logical positivism and its offspring logical empiricism—the final denouement actually bore witness to the collapse of the
would-be philosophical assassins and the rescue of normative thinking
on social and political topics. Far from dead, normative analysis is currently being applied to a range of practical concerns—biomedicine, law,
the professions, and a host of public policy issues—something that would
have been unimaginable at the time of Weldon's pronouncement. As this
list lengthens, philosophers have been working to articulate the bases of
normative analysis.

   This chapter represents an effort to foster awareness of the need for
more and stronger normative analyses in evaluation practice and of the
important role that the concept of social justice, and normative theories
of social justice, has to play in the evaluation of social programs, practices, policies, and institutions. The first part of this chapter considers
some reasons for why evaluators have been wary about applying social
justice concerns to evaluation practice. The second part reviews the formal concept of social justice and several substantive theories of justice
that have been developed within the liberal tradition. The third applies
some of the results of this review to the situation of the educational
system as a whole in our society.

NEW DIRECTIONS FOR PROGRAM EVALUATION, no. 45, Spring 1990 © Jossey-Bass Inc., Publishers

## Social Justice and the Evaluation Community

"Justice," writes the liberal philosopher John Rawls (1971), "is the first virtue of social institutions, as truth is [of] systems of thought" (p. 3). Of ancient lineage, this ideal has played an especially central role in the modern era of social protest and reconstruction. Invoked by those who would decry and transform the basic structures and practices of society, it functions both as a vision of a future in which human exploitation and manipulation are forever banished and as a more mundane critical standard by which to gauge the health of day-to-day social practice.

As such, it might be thought that social justice is a, if not the, central moral standard that practitioners of evaluation readily apply to social programs, practices, and institutions. And yet, with the exception of those who have at times advocated "judgmental" models of evaluation (for example, Scriven, House, and Stake), the evaluation field in general has refrained from commenting on the justice of the practices being evaluated.

This phenomenon is puzzling, for as the general term *evaluation* suggests, an evaluator is concerned with determining the value or worth of a social program or practice. There is fairly widespread agreement within evaluation circles that such is evaluation's role. Indeed, because the gauging of value is central to the practice of evaluation, many evaluators would claim that this aspect of their activities distinguishes evaluation from research. But if so, why is there so little comment by evaluators on the justice of social programs, policies, and practices?

There are a number of reasons for this general reticence. First, there is the political context of evaluation practice. Second, there is the view that the practice of evaluation extends only to cover social programs, policies, and practices, not to institutions (the *true* subject of social justice) in which the former are merely embedded. And third, despite the intent to determine the value and worth of a program, evaluators generally disclaim any responsibility for judging the ends or aims of the programs.

*The Context of Evaluation Is Political.* Evaluation practice often occurs in a socially charged atmosphere in which participants and stakeholders have conflicting views. In judging whether a practice or program does or does not conform to certain standards of social justice, evaluators may feel that they risk (1) alienating many of their various audiences, (2) adding to the explosiveness of a situation, (3) undermining the utility of the evaluation, and (4) undermining their own credibility as objective arbiters. It is true that a program's contribution to social injustice has far more emotive impact than mere program failure. Nonetheless, in adhering to evaluation standards that prescribe evaluator sensitivity to the "needs" of various constituencies and to the actual distribution of program benefits and burdens, evaluators are often in the best position to judge when the requirements of justice are ignored. To ignore inequities demeans both the virtues of courage and integrity that is a key part of evaluation demands. It may be that a program successfully achieves its goals, but that the goals are reprehensible.

*Social Justice Applies Only to Institutions.* The *Standards of Evaluations of Educational Programs, Projects, and Materials* (Stufflebeam, 1981) explicitly state that these standards do not apply to evaluations of institutions. If social justice is therefore a concept applying only to institutions, it may be that evaluators do not operate in a framework that allows for social justice considerations. Beyond the false assumption that programs and policies cannot be just or unjust, this view of the proper object of evaluation is unduly restrictive. Programs and practices are embedded within institutions and, as such, are influenced by the institutional environment—the structures, roles, and relations that are constitutive of the institutions. In the worst case, it is like evaluating the success of a new training program in a slave-owning society without pausing to consider the relationship of the program to the institution of slavery. Just as programs and policies can be just and unjust in their own right, the injustice of an institution can pervade its attendant programs and practices in a way that glaringly reveals the pretense that evaluation can be merely confined to them. We shall explore an example of this when we examine the social justice of the educational system in the third part.

*Value Judgments Are Subjective.* Many evaluators are unwilling to make social justice arguments on the grounds that these claims are inherently subjective and not rationally determinable. These evaluators view their task as merely to determine whether a program is causally efficacious in reaching its goals (or "goal-free" evaluation, in determining intended and unintended consequences). No judgment about the worthiness of the goals or the moral appropriateness of the means is made. However, this view rests on the now-discredited tenets of logical positivism and empiricism, philosophical approaches that formed the conceptual frameworks within which many evaluators and social scientists were trained. Key to these approaches was an attempt to drive a logical wedge between empirical and value claims. Only the former were the subject of science and could be rationally justified, while value claims were banished to the realm of subjectivity.

This purported distinction succumbed to the view that social inquiry necessarily presupposes evaluative elements in a holistic network of relations so that they pervade even the most low-level empirical claims (Taylor, 1967; Hesse, 1978; Thomas, 1979). Thus we can speak of social science and inquiry claims as being only more or less empirical or more or less evaluative.

Moreover, the logical empiricist account was never able to overcome the objection that the very concepts used in social inquiry are themselves value laden (consider the moral understandings that form part of the concept of a teacher); they presuppose a network of evaluative social practices that themselves arise out of a practical interest in securing the good and desirable in human affairs. This challenge has not led to a morass of subjectivity and irrationality; instead, recent philosophical analyses demonstrate how complex, intricate, and even exacting are the forms of moral reasoning. Such analysis belies the notion that evaluative judgments are the expression of mere personal preference, and thus, evaluators need not fear bringing considerations of social justice into the practice of evaluation. Indeed, considering that a typical evaluation situation in part involves the identification of distributions of benefits and burdens and the principles from which they issue, it is far-fetched and potentially self-deceiving even to believe that such is possible. It remains to consider briefly some systematic accounts of social justice.

## Liberal Conceptions of Social Justice

*The Concept of Formal Social Justice.* There are different varieties of justice, among them political, criminal, corrective, and social justice. Our concern is this chapter is only with the latter: social justice. The widely agreed-on scope of social justice is the fair distribution of social and economic benefits and liabilities within a social or public context. Aristotle identified it well when he noted that social justice is receiving one's due; injustice is receiving more or less than one's due. Social justice, whether it applies to the individual or to a group, implies a relationship among social beings that involves a distribution of social and economic goods in virtue of some aspect or condition of the individual or group in question. Social justice thus involves a principle(s) of distribution (it is not aggregative); that is, the determination of shares of some total amount of goods (Barry, 1965). Second, social justice requires the distribution of social and economic benefits and burdens, such as positions, income, and status (rather than, say, civil liberties—the subject of political justice). Third, such a distribution is based on some property or condition of an individual (or group), for example, needs or contributions. And fourth, it suggests a principle of proportionality; that is, if the property or condition forming the basis of the distribution can be quantified, then social justice requires that each receive a share corresponding to the relative amount of that property or condition. Social justice as a formal concept does not therefore require a strictly equal division of goods as some egalitarians have argued (see Miller, 1976, for a fuller discussion).

The formal principle of social justice cannot be used to determine the appropriate distribution of goods, since it merely establishes the scope and formal conditions that any substantive principles of social justice must meet. Substantive principles of social justice are those that identify the relevant property or condition of individuals (or groups) that is to form the basis of the distribution of social and economic benefits and burdens. Thus, we can imagine a society that selects red hair and blue eyes as substantive principles of social justice. In such a society, those with very red hair and very blue eyes will do exceedingly well in the social and economic payout. Those with lesser amounts of these properties will do correspondingly worse. However, we would object to this type of social arrangement, for it is hard to see how hair and eye color can determine how well the person does in society. Such a situation seems unjust.

This point implies that not just any property or condition can be an adequate substantive principle of social justice, even though it might pass the formal tests for a conception of social justice. Substantive principles must also pass certain normative and moral tests. Thus it is the function of normative moral and social analysis to argue for the nature of the criteria that form such tests and to show why a certain property or condition passes (or fails to pass) the criteria in question and so form morally acceptable (or unacceptable) principles of social justice.

Within the liberal tradition, three main, systematic accounts of social justice have been offered in recent times: utilitarianism, John Rawls's theory of justice as fairness, and Robert Nozick's libertarian theory of justice. (It must be stated here that there is controversy over whether utilitarianism is a liberal theory of social justice at all.) Each of these theories has argued that principles of social justice must pass certain criteria, and each argues that although none of the others passes the tests, their own favored principles of social justice do. These accounts are explored below, since this discussion will further our treatment of the educational system in the next part and since these are relevant accounts of social justice for the evaluation community to consider in the context of evaluation practice.

*Utilitarianism and Social Justice.* Utilitarianism is a comprehensive moral theory, and is divided into several distinct types, depending, in part, on its attitude toward social justice. As a teleological moral theory, utilitarianism characteristically defines moral rightness in terms of moral goodness, or as that which maximizes the good. The good here is to be understood as happiness (or pleasure or utility), which is defined independently of moral rightness. Moral rightness is simply that which maximizes happiness or utility (either in terms of total welfare or else in terms of average welfare per capita). The other main kind of moral theory is nonteleological (or deontological), in that the moral rightness of an action, policy, or institution is defined independently of the good. As we shall see, both Rawls's and Nozick's theories are deontological and oppose utilitarianism on the grounds that maximizing utility may often conflict with the dictates of justice.

*Social Justice as a Problem for Utilitarianism.* The concept of social justice has long presented something of a problem for utilitarianism, because utilitarianism is an aggregative theory; that is, it measures actions or practices in terms of the total (or average per capita) welfare produced. Social justice, on the other hand, focuses solely on the distribution of some aggregate, as noted earlier. Whereas utilitarianism seems to imply that an action is right if and only if it creates a greater net sum of utility than any other alternative, social justice is concerned with the moral appropriateness of the distribution of utilities and disutilities (or benefits and burdens, however defined) among individuals or groups. Thus if social justice is of great importance in our moral universe, as it seems to be, then utilitarianism seems to be challenged as an acceptable moral theory.

*The Utilitarian Response.* Utilitarians have responded to this challenge in a variety of ways. First, many argue that a strict utilitarian must be uncompromising on the principle that the maximization of total (or average) utility is what is morally right—that such maximization is the one and only moral test. Thus concerns about the distribution of benefits are given no or, at best, little consideration. Utilitarianism, it is often held, was developed to bring order, consistency, and coherence to our considered moral judgments. So if social justice requires a focus on distribution, then social justice and our esteem of it must be discarded, not the principle of utility.

*Import for Evaluation.* This tough-minded response may account for why the evaluation field has generally failed to include considerations of social justice. Certain general notions of utilitarianism have been incorporated into welfare economics and help form the conceptual foundations of cost-benefit analysis—tools and principles that have been carried over into evaluation. Thus, consciously or not, many evaluators have focused on determining the overall benefits of programs rather than the patterns of distribution within programs. This utilitarian legacy of evaluation no longer fits with the now-prevalent view within the evaluation community that evaluators should be sensitive to the various needs of stakeholders. This stance implies that a distributive point of view is also necessary within evaluation and provides further reason that evaluators should be concerned with social justice issues.

*Other Utilitarian Responses.* Rather than dispensing with social justice, another group of utilitarians continues to view it as having high moral import. Rather than abandoning the principle of utility when it conflicts with the idea of appropriate distribution, these philosophers attempt to incorporate justice within a utilitarian framework, which, in part, has led to the distinction between act and rule utilitarianism. While act utilitarianism retains a unitary principle of utility, rule utilitarians argue that a variety of moral principles—including social justice—may be applied to cases. (This is not to imply that social justice cannot be assessed within an act utilitarian framework. For a recent attempt, see Smart [1978]. Rather, social justice is less likely to be viewed as a major issue within act utilitarianism.) For example, Mill (1961 [1861]) viewed justice as an important moral value, but he justified the overriding importance of justice in terms of its tendency to maximize utility. Thus, the principle of utility remained the supreme test.

*Problems with Utilitarianism.* Utilitarianism in whatever form has come under fire from both philosophers and economists. Utilitarianism suffers from the requirement that different individuals' utilities (the aggregate of which equals total welfare) can be commonly measured and compared (that is, "cardinal" utility measurements). Yet economists have argued that such interpersonal utility schedules cannot, in principle, be made. (The extent to which this objection depends on the discredited verificationism of logical empiricism is discussed by Barry, 1989, pp. 104–107.) Even if this objection can be nullified, it is still unclear and controversial as to how such measurements (or their indirect substitutes, such as Pareto movements) can be made.

Moreover, the information "costs" necessary to determining the net sum of utilities (arrived at by subtracting disutilities) for a program or a decision can be immense. This also points to another problem faced by evaluators enamored with the notion of stakeholders. There seems to be no nonarbitrary way to determine who the relevant parties are in making utility calculations (which calculations could extend to future generations).

However, the fundamental objection to utilitarianism arises out of its seeming inability to recognize persons, rather than their preferences, as the distinct locus of moral value. For utilitarianism, it is the maximization of total welfare that matters, not the treatment of the individual. Thus if the greatest net welfare is maximized through social arrangements that require a portion of the population to be enslaved, then utilitarianism would hold that slavery is morally right and morally required. Utilitarianism is ultimately incompatible with the Kantian imperative of moral individualism that forms the moral basis of liberalism: Persons should always be treated as ends in themselves and never merely as means. For the liberal, the individual is morally prior to any conception of the good life or any possible social arrangements. As the locus of moral value, the priority of the individual places constraints on the pursuit of the good and the way institutions may be developed.

Hence, even if Mill had been able to show that just institutions promote the general welfare, such a conclusion is merely contingent on and relative to the prevailing natural and social conditions. Change either or both, and the principle of utility may require that some persons be treated as merely tools to maximize the general (or average) utility.

Both Rawls and Nozick, who claim to be Kant's heirs, have forcefully objected to utilitarianism on these grounds as well as the further grounds that persons, as choosers of ends, are prior to whatever ends they ultimately decide on. It is not preferences that morally matter but rather the chooser of ends: the person.

*Justice as Fairness or Libertarianism?* In perhaps the most celebrated statement of normative moral theory of this century, Rawls has reinvested the Kantian view of justice shorn of Kant's "transcendental" metaphysics. Rather than locating the person as chooser beyond the domain of the temporal and physical world as Kant did, Rawls seeks to place the person within a recognizable human situation. As Rawls (1980, p. 522) states:

> Justice as fairness begins from the idea that the most appropriate conception of justice for the basic structure of a democratic society is one that its citizens would adopt in a situation that is fair between them and in which they are represented as free and equal moral persons. This situation is the original position: we conjecture that the fairness of the circumstances under which agreement is reached transfers to the principles of justice agreed to. . . . Thus the name: "justice as fairness."

In other words, Rawls would have us imagine a situation ("the original position") in which a number of rational, self-interested persons under natural conditions of moderate scarcity ("the circumstances of justice") come together to decide on the principles that will underlie their society. Though they do not know in advance what principles they will choose, they do know that such a choice would be preferable to a condition of "general egoism" (better to hang together than each going his or her way). Thus Rawls claims that justice should be mutually advantageous. Although these individuals know general facts about the human condition, Rawls casts over them a "veil of ignorance" so that they know nothing about their particular circumstances (for example, sex, race, intelligence, or what their position in society would be under varying principles of justice). The veil is designed to ensure that the bargaining situation is equalized for all parties. Moreover, these persons are endowed with a modicum of concern for their descendants.

Under these conditions, Rawls (1971, p. 302) attempts to show that such representative, rational, self-interested bargainers would choose the following two principles:

1. Each person is to have an equal right to the most extensive total system of equal basic liberties compatible with a similar system of liberties for all.

2. Social and economic inequalities are to be arranged so that they

are both: (a) to the greatest benefit of the least advantaged, consistent with the just savings principle, and (b) attached to offices and positions open to all under conditions of fair equality of opportunity.

Rawls provides a lexical ordering to these two principles so that the first principle (equal liberties) receives priority over the second. In this way, he argues that it could never be just to trade a greater level of general welfare for a system of unequal liberties. Within the second principle, which arranges for social and economic inequalities, part b—the fair equality of opportunity principle—takes lexical priority over part a—what Rawls calls the difference principle.

In what follows, I shall focus attention only on the second principle, since it alone provides Rawls's view of social justice. The first principle, though presupposed in this discussion, is a principle of political justice. In addition, I ignore the "just savings" clause, designed to ensure adequate future investment, of the second principle. And finally, I shall frame the discussion without further concern for the relation between the original position and the two principles (see Sandel, 1982, and Barry, 1989, for the justification of this approach). Since Nozick takes exception to Rawls at key points, we shall be able to see what divides liberal egalitarianism from libertarianism.

*The Difference Principle.* Rawls's egalitarianism is embedded in his view of the difference principle. Though the difference principle permits social and economic inequalities, it does so only if such inequalities benefit the socially and economically least advantaged in society. (Rawls does not intend *the least advantaged* to refer to specific individuals in a society. Rather, the term refers to a social category, such as the category of individuals falling below half the median level of income and wealth. See Barry [1973, ch. 5] for further discussion.) In his defense of this principle, Rawls (1971, ch. 2) examines three possible arrangements for distributing social and economic benefits: (1) natural liberty, (2) liberal equality, and (3) democratic equality.

1. *Natural liberty*, roughly the libertarian position espoused by Nozick, understands social justice to be achieved when distributions of benefits result from the workings of a free (market) economy in which formal equality of opportunity exists (positions and offices are open to all with the requisite talent). Here the state plays a minimal role of "night watchman" and is nonredistributionist in its treatment of income. As long as individuals observe the rights of others, they are entitled to keep whatever their talents can bring in the market.

2. *Liberal equality*, or fair meritocracy, is in Rawls's view an improvement on a system of natural liberty. Unlike natural liberty, the liberal equality view recognizes that inequalities emerge out of the structure of society. Individuals of equal ability and motivation may end up with different outcomes owing to their differing initial starting points in

society. Thus, if race, sex, and class actually hinder the attainment of success, formal equality of opportunity is insufficient to achieve social justice. Because race, sex, and class are morally irrelevant to what one deserves, social justice requires that these barriers be eliminated through a redistributive provision of resources (income transfers, special programs of education, affirmative action) to ensure that only native talent and determination win out. Here inequalities are justified only if there exists initially fair conditions for all (part b of Rawls's second principle).

3. *Democratic equality*, based on Rawls's (1971) difference principle, argues that a fair meritocracy is actually an unjust system of distribution because "it still permits the distribution of wealth and income to be determined by the *natural* distribution of abilities and talents" (p. 73, emphasis added). Rawls's insight here is if being born into a certain social class is morally irrelevant, then so is being born with certain abilities. Because no one deserves their standing in the "natural lottery," natural abilities and native determination cannot form a morally permissible basis for distributing social and economic goods. Once both social and natural conditions of individuals are seen to be wholly accidental, no basis remains for some to be more deserving than others. Social justice thus seems to demand strict equality of outcomes.

As Rawls's difference principle suggests, however, he is not content to leave matters there. He recognizes that a strictly equal society provides a disincentive to working hard and long. Such a society could end up with all having equal shares of misery. (As Barry [1989] points out, Rawls has to assume that the society arising out of the original position is mutually preferable to the results of nonagreement among such self-interested, rational individuals. Barry rightly points out the difficulties this creates for Rawls's theory.) Thus he allows for social and economic inequalities on the grounds that they are incentives for the talented. Such inequalities are permissible, because those worst off will be better off with the incentive system than without it. Thus the least advantaged have no rational or moral cause for complaint. While those who do well under this scheme do not deserve such premiums, they are entitled to them. (Contrary to Miller, 1976, the difference principle does satisfy the formal requirements of social justice—to each his due—since entitlements to positions can be earned through superior educational attainment.) But all entitlements arise only out of agreement on the cooperative form of society that maximizes the benefits of those worst off and do not antedate the existence of such an agreement, as traditional principles of desert have been interpreted (see Feinberg, 1970).

*Nozick's Counter.* Following Sandel (1982, p. 77), we can understand Nozick's libertarian counterattack as focusing on two key points in Rawls's argument. The first concerns Rawls's view of persons and their relation to their attributes, which allows Rawls to derive the difference principle and to view individuals' talents and abilities as possessions of the community rather than of the individuals. The second argues for a system of natural liberty by attacking Rawls's argument against desert.

First, Nozick (1974) questions Rawls's liberal credentials by raising the question: What is left of a person once stripped of personal traits? Nozick implies that such an approach is illiberal. In considering the abilities of individuals as common property of the society to be used in the service of those worst off will we not be treating those naturally best off merely as means and not as ends—a clear violation of the liberal principle of respect for persons? Thus the entirety of Rawls's defense of the difference principle rests on the coherence of Rawls's view of a person, which turns real individuals strongly situated and "thick with traits" into apparently disembodied egos. For only that (incoherent?) conception could preserve Rawls's distinction between" it's not *really me* who is being used, it's just my assets."

Sandel (1982) argues that Rawls is confounded at this point and argues that only the abandonment of liberalism can save his theory. "If the difference principle is to avoid using some as means to others' ends, it can only be possible under circumstances where the subject of posses-sion [of a person's assets] is a 'we' rather than 'I,' which circumstances imply in turn the existence of a community in the constitutive sense [of what a person is]" (p. 80). Here Sandel points the way toward evaluating basic societal institutions from a communitarian standpoint (for example, see Bellah and others, 1985). (I have not chosen to comment on communitarianism, since that would involve us in deep issues of philosophy of mind as well as social philosophy [see Stoutland, 1990, for an excellent discussion.] The Sirotnik and Oakes contribution in this volume draws partly from a critical theory tradition that is embedded within a kind of communitarianism.)

Nozick's second line of attack concerns Rawls's inference from the point that "no one deserves their native talents and abilities" to "no one deserves or is entitled to the benefits these talents produce." As Nozick (1974) notes: "Some of the things [native talent] he uses he just may *have*, not illegitimately. It needn't be that the foundations underlying desert are themselves deserved, all the way down" (p. 225). Rawls's consistent response here is to say that this argument misses the point, since it is not the case that a person possesses abilities in the requisite way to be deserving.

Once more Rawls relies on his view of a person as being only accidentally connected to his or her characteristics. In anticipating this defense, Nozick replies that even if a person does not own his or her characteristics, it does not follow that society does. For if individuals do not possess their characteristics, then at best we can say that no one— including society—possesses them. Since abilities are not like "manna from heaven" that fall where they may, but come attached only to individuals, the presumption of how they are to be used and for whose benefit they are used is with the individual, not society. Thus, even if they are not deserved, individuals are entitled to whatever social and economic benefits flow from the use of their abilities.

Rawls at this point appears unable to establish the difference principle since, as Nozick shows, he is unable to establish the inference from individual nonownership of abilities to community ownership. But does it follow, then, that Nozick is right that the libertarian position concerning just entitlement wins out? It does not follow. For, as Rawls rightly points out, entitlement is different from desert. Whereas deserts precede the founding of social institutions, entitlements can only be created with the original agreement on the basic structure of society. If there is no such thing as preexisting deserts that society is duty bound to recognize, then individuals are entitled to deserts only if a legitimate social decision is so made. For Rawls the only legitimate social decision is one that works to the advantage of those least well off. The argument seems deadlocked.

## Evaluating the Educational System

Although we appear to have reached an impasse in our discussion of which substantive principles of social justice are morally preferable, it seems to be merely a temporary impasse. Nonetheless, we can use the gains made in clarifying these approaches to examine the structure and dynamics of the educational system as it applies to social justice issues. (The discussion of the distributive nature of the educational system that follows is elaborated in Green, Ericson, and Seidman [1980]. I have addressed issues of social justice concerning the distributive nature of the educational system in depth in Ericson and Robertshaw [1982] and Ericson [1987].) For here we can see exactly how social justice issues can be raised in evaluating the system and the programs within it.

*The Distributive Behavior of the Educational System.* Adopting once more the distributive point of view natural to the concept of social justice, it is fruitful to view the educational system as in part a system of distribution. Just as the social and economic system distributes benefits and liabilities to individuals and groups, so does the educational system. Although economic resources are allocated to the educational system and these are distributed by the educational system to its various levels and programs through a variety of decision processes, I am not here referring to the allocation and distribution of economic goods. Why is it that battles over the amount of resources to be allocated to the educational system often become so heated? The issue is not how much education (as opposed to health, welfare, and other major programs) should receive but rather that resources produce and spread educational achievement. That is, the educational system is our society's primary mechanism for distributing the benefits of education: knowledge, skill, standards of civility, and the like.

Yet, the educational system, though relatively independent (see Green, Ericson, and Seidman, 1980; and Ericson, 1982), is not an island unto itself. It is interlocked with other major social institutions, specifically the social and economic system that generates the distribution of social and economic benefits and liabilities. What is important is not that the educational system is interlocked with the social and economic system but how it is interlocked. For example, it might be that the two are connected but the nature of the connection is such that issues of social justice that arise for the social and economic system have no application to the distributive mechanism of the educational system, and vice versa. This would be the case if the distribution of educational benefits by the educational system had no bearing on the subsequent distribution of social and economic benefits, or in other words, that education had no bearing on life opportunities. Of course this is not the case. Education clearly impacts life chances. Thus the distributive system of the educational system is powerfully connected to the distributive system of the social and economic system. For this reason, as well as the fact that educational benefits can be viewed as a kind of social benefit, the distributive behavior of the educational system is deeply connected with issues of social justice.

*The Distributive Connection Defined.* In the most basic, abstract, and unqualified form (for full accounts, see Green, Ericson, and Seidman, 1980; and Ericson, 1987), the distributive behavior of the educational system and its link to the social and economic system is actually composed of four distinct distributions and their attendant mechanisms: (1) the distribution of educationally relevant attributes (ability, tenacity, and choice), (2) the distribution of educational benefits (knowledge, skills, and so on), (3) the distribution of surrogate educational benefits (grades, degrees, letters of recommendation), and (4) the distribution of noneducational social and economic benefits (positions, status, income, and the like). Of these four distributions, only two items—2 and 3—are distributed directly by the educational system. The distribution of educationally relevant attributes is done throughout the population by the natural lottery and by one's early childhood social situation. The distribution of social and economic benefits is made by the social and economic system. Within each distribution, there can be and are inequalities among individuals and groups in the relative possession of each particular attribute or good. What is important is that these inequalities are transmitted from one distribution to the next. In other words, they are serially connected. This is to say, the distribution of educationally relevant attributes in the school-age population (which is likely to be highly unequal among individuals and between groups) in large part gives rise to the distribution of educational benefits in that same population (some learn more than others). In turn, the distribution of educational benefits ideally produces a distribution of surrogate educational benefits (some get higher grades, higher test scores, higher degrees, or better recommendations than others). (See Ericson [1984] for a discussion of the issues created when the second and third distributions are viewed as misaligned.) Finally, the distribution of social and economic benefits (some get better jobs, earn more, obtain higher status than others) is distributed on the basis of the distribution of surrogate educational benefits.

*A Desert-Based Educational Meritocracy.* Wittingly or not, what we have largely created in our society in this century is an educational system-based, meritocratic society. (I say in large part because we also have an entitlement system that allows wealth, if not status, to be passed from parent to offspring.) Central to the arrangement is the notion that social and economic advantages and disadvantages should be based on the distribution of surrogate educational benefits. *On the basis* here entails more than an empirical likelihood of a positive relation between the two distributions. Rather, it has to do with the manner in which the distribution of social and economic benefits is socially legitimated. As Green, Ericson, and Seidman (1980) put it, what is entailed is the following normative principle connecting the educational system to the social and economic system: "Those having a greater share of surrogate educational benefits deserve [or at least are entitled to] a greater share of social and economic benefits" (p. 43). This educational system-based, meritocratic principle thus provides a social basis for regarding social and economic inequalities as justified. In other words, it is a clear principle of social justice.

*Social Justice and the Educational System.* In light of our discussion of principles of social justice, it should be clear that the operative distributive principle of the educational system is very close to the view of the libertarian, "natural liberty" position in which individuals deserve, or at least are entitled to, whatever they can command in the market under conditions of formal equality of opportunity. Education here is seen as talent development (human capital investment) or of investing in one's own future in the competition for the best (educationally qualified) social positions. Yet this position differs in two ways from the full-blown libertarian view, since this stance is established within a public system of education and moves somewhat beyond the principle of formal equality of opportunity. Libertarians, unless they regard education as a duty to forestall individuals becoming criminal threats to property holders, should be inclined to view education as a matter left for individual choice to be pursued through a system of private providers unsubsidized by the state. Moreover, since some programs for the socially disadvantaged are provided, the principle of educational meritocracy operates in an environment that does at least pay lip service to Rawls's principle of fair equality of opportunity. To implement fully the principle of fair equality of opportunity, however, would require that a disproportionately high amount of economic and educational resources be provided for the socially and economically disadvantaged. Thus though we recognize the ideal implicit in fair equality, our actual practice is much closer to the principle of formal equality.

Even though our society rejects, in principle, a utilitarian-type arrangement that seeks to maximize total welfare by lavishing on those most endowed with educationally relevant attributes the major share of economic and educational resources, we are clearly at odds with Rawls's difference principle that regards inequalities distributed on the basis of the natural lottery to be morally arbitrary and not permissible. Indeed, our society positively embraces the natural lottery as a basis for distributing social and economic advantages and disadvantages.

Thus the social justice of the educational system turns on the moral adequacy of the natural liberty view, or a Rawlsian theory of justice (or a communitarian version of it), assuming that utilitarianism and fair equality (because it is hard to stop there) are noncompetitive views. However, we have seen, though the consequences are large, the arguments are difficult and intricate.

## Conclusion

Whether examining a curriculum, a large-scale educational program, or the institution of education itself, evaluators must be sensitive to concerns of social justice. All educational practices are subject to the distributive dynamics of the educational system, which allots educational benefits in an unequal manner. Thus an evaluation that simply attempts to identify in a summative or formative manner actual or likely program consequences is necessarily incomplete. This is a strong reminder that evaluation practice cannot escape the necessity of raising and dealing with the normative and ethical concerns naturally embedded within educational practice. To pretend that such escape is possible equates to a posture that has little moral justification. Evaluators must acknowledge to their audience their position on issues of social justice, whether libertarian, meritocratic, egalitarian, or otherwise.

Regardless of the social justice stance, evaluations should be conducted within a framework where these individuals or groups benefiting or not benefiting are identified. Evaluations should also be conducted with an attempt at identifying the mechanism of distribution. Even a lip-service endorsement of the principle of fair equality of opportunity, as now exists within our society, argues that evaluators should seek to ensure that (potentially) morally arbitrary and irrelevant attributes of individuals (such as race, sex, ethnicity, and the like) are not the operative mechanisms in generating distributions of educational benefits. Although it is difficult to decide the ultimate issue of social justice, it is clearly possible for evaluators to adopt the distributive point of view. Though social justice requires much more than this, it morally commands no less.

## References

Barry, B. *Political Argument*. London: Routledge & Kegan Paul, 1965.

Barry, B. *The Liberal Theory of Justice*. Oxford, England: Clarendon Press, 1973.

Barry, B. *Theories of Justice*. Berkeley: University of California Press, 1989.

Bellah, R. N., Madsen, R., Sullivan, W., Swidler, A., and Tipton, S. *Habits of the Heart*. New York: Harper & Row, 1985.

Ericson, D. P. "The Possibility of a General Theory of the Educational System." In M. Archer (ed.), *The Sociology of Educational Expansion*. Newbury Park, Calif.: Sage, 1982.

Ericson, D. P. "Of Minima and Maxima: The Social Significance of Minimal Competency Testing and the Search for Educational Excellence." *American Journal of Education*, 1984, *92* (3), 245–261.

Ericson, D. P. "Justice and Compulsion in the Educational System." Unpublished article, Graduate School of Education, University of California, Los Angeles, 1987.

Ericson, D. P., and Robertshaw, D. "Social Justice and the Community College." *Community/Junior College Quarterly of Research and Practice*, 1982, *6* (4), 315–342.

Feinberg, J. *Doing and Deserving*. Princeton, N.J.: Princeton University Press, 1970.

Green, T. F., with Ericson, D. P., and Seidman, R. H. *Predicting the Behavior of the Educational System*. Syracuse, N.Y.: Syracuse University Press, 1980.

Hesse, M. "Theory and Value in the Social Sciences." In C. Hookway and P. Pettit (eds.), *Action and Interpretation*. Cambridge, England: Cambridge University Press, 1978.

Mill, J. S. *Utilitarianism*. Garden City, N.Y.: Doubleday, 1961. (Originally published 1861.)

Miller, D. *Social Justice*. Oxford, England: Clarendon Press, 1976.

Nozick, R. *Anarchy, State, and Utopia*. New York: Basic Books, 1974.

Rawls, J. *A Theory of Justice*. Cambridge, Mass.: Harvard University Press, 1971.

Rawls, J. "Kantian Constructivism in Moral Theory: The Dewey Lectures." *Journal of Philosophy*, 1980, *77*, 515–572.

Sandel, M. *Liberalism and the Limits of Justice*. Cambridge, England: Cambridge University Press, 1982.

Smart, J.J.C. "Distributive Justice and Utilitarianism." In J. Arthur and W. H. Shaw (eds.), *Justice and Economic Distribution*. Englewood Cliffs, N.J.: Prentice-Hall, 1978.

Stoutland, F. "Self and Society in the Claims of Individualism." *Studies in Philosophy and Education*, forthcoming.

Stufflebeam, D. (chair), and the Joint Committee on Standards for Educational Evaluation. *Standards for Evaluations of Educational Programs, Projects, and Materials*. New York: McGraw-Hill, 1981.

Taylor, C. "Neutrality in Political Science." In P. Laslett and W. G. Runciman (eds.), *Philosophy, Politics, and Society.* (3rd series.) Oxford, England: Oxford University Press, 1967.

Thomas, D. *Naturalism and Social Science.* Cambridge, England: Cambridge University Press, 1979.

*David P. Ericson is associate professor of philosophy of education in the Graduate School of Education, University of California, Los Angeles. He is currently working on two books on the logic of inquiry in education and the nature of causal inference in the social sciences. He is also editor-in-chief of* Studies in Philosophy and Education.

*Evaluation methodology itself has sometimes led, in complex
and subtle ways, to systematic injustices. The main source of
error lies in our standard conception of causation, which is
inadequate and incorrect.*

# Methodology and Justice

*Ernest R. House*

No problem is more difficult and complex in the social sciences than
that of how values are embedded within the research methodologies that
we employ. That values should and must exist in research is no longer
denied. In fact, we actively encourage and promote values such as objectivity, impartiality, fairness, and efficiency. Other values, such as partiality,
we try to curtail as much as possible, and our failure to do so constitutes
bias. Many values, however, remain implicit rather than explicit in our
work, hidden in ways not discernible, even to ourselves, and while these
embedded values may not be harmful or wrong, sometimes they are both.
Although it is easy to discern certain values in our work, analyzing
research methodology itself presents a particularly difficult problem, since
we believe that we are protected from bias by our methods. Indeed, that is
why we employ them.

Social justice is among the most important values we should hope
to secure in evaluation studies. The contemporary practice of evaluation
is part of the political authority structure of society, and evaluation as
an aid to public decision making entails conceptions of democracy and
social justice, even when these conceptions are not immediately apparent.
Public evaluation should be an institution for democratizing public decision making, for making decisions, programs, and policies more open
to public scrutiny and deliberation. As an institutionalized practice, it
should conform to the values and ethics of a democratic society. Considerations such as justice, impartiality, and equality, while subject to

I wish to thank Sandra M. Mathison and Kenneth Howe for making helpful
comments on an earlier draft of this chapter.

disagreement and debate on their exact meaning, are neither arbitrary nor relative.

Evaluations should serve the interests not only of the sponsor but of the larger society and of various groups within society, particularly those most affected by the program under review. Hence, as a social practice, evaluation entails an inescapable ethic of public responsibility, responsibility that extends well beyond the immediate client. Social justice in evaluation, then, concerns the manner in which various interests are served. (By interests, I mean that which is conducive to the achievement of individuals' wants, needs, or purposes; needs are anything necessary to the survival or well-being of individuals.) To be free is to know one's interests and to possess the desire and the ability and resources—the power and opportunity—to move toward these interests.

## Craniometry: A Lesson of History

History contains stories of grave injustices perpetrated by leading scientists operating with what they thought to be the best research methods of their day. Nineteenth-century craniometry provides a dramatic example. Operating from the presumption (based on animal studies) that larger brains meant more intelligence, nineteenth-century scientists developed methods to measure the brain sizes of humans, and thus to measure the intelligence they thought brain size indicated. Leading scientists of the day, such as physician Samuel George Morton of Philadelphia and Paul Broca, professor of surgery and founder of the Anthropological Society of Paris, developed precise methods for estimating brain size, usually by weighing the brain or by measuring cranial volume (Gould, 1981).

In the latter technique, the skull of the (deceased) subject was filled with lead shot, following procedures carefully prescribed as to what type of shot to use, how the shot should be tamped down, what kind of container the shot should be transferred to, and how the shot should be measured. Craniometricians estimated skull capacity with increasing precision and objectivity, carefully recording minute differences among groups of people all over the world. The results of such studies were that Caucasians had larger brains than other races and that men had larger brains than women—exactly what these scientists had hypothesized from the start since, in popular opinion, whites were more intelligent than other races and men were more intelligent than women. These findings appeared not only in technical journals but also flooded the popular press (Gould, 1981). In 1981 noted geologist Stephen Jay Gould studied these nineteenth-century craniometric studies in detail and concluded in *The Mismeasure of Man* that precision of measurement and objectivity in method could never overcome the inherent racism and sexism implicit in the beginning assumptions themselves, a bias the scientists of that day never recognized. Broca, one of the leading scientists of his day, started with the assumption that the human races could be ranked on a linear scale of mental worth and explored any indices that he thought might yield the proper ranking. The craniometricians asserted the objectivity of their findings on the basis of the careful precision of their measurements and repeatedly explained away inconsistencies.

For example, when craniometricians claimed that German men had larger brains than Frenchmen, Broca eliminated the measured differences by considerations of age and body size, since older and smaller people have smaller brains. But he did not use the same correction for the differences between men and women. When it turned out that many prominent men who had donated their brains to these studies had small- or average-sized brains, Broca reasoned that the men were small in stature or were elderly when they died. At one point he hinted that the work of some of these men was not as eminent as claimed. He could not know that his own brain was only slightly above average in size. Although craniometry seems ludicrous now, gross injustices were perpetrated on vast numbers of people by this research.

By this extreme example I do not mean to imply that we have corresponding problems in the contemporary practice of evaluation. The evaluation examples cited here do not begin to approach the crass injustices of craniometry. Fortunately, we start from a higher plateau of moral sensitivity, and the injustices emerging from current evaluation methods are far less severe—but they are also far more subtle.

From Gould's analysis of craniometry, I draw two conclusions: First, the complexity and careful precision of research methods is no guarantee of their impartiality. Second, the intellectual and ideological climate of the age can seriously affect how studies are conducted and what conclusions are drawn, in spite of objective methodology. I focus in this chapter on methodological concerns, having dealt with the ideological context elsewhere (House, in press). Obvious contaminations of our methods, such as coercion, dishonesty, and falsification, I ignore. It is the potential injustice of our best methods that I wish to explore.

## Two Evaluation Examples

In what follows I present two examples in evaluation where justice was not done: the evaluations of Follow Through and PUSH/Excel. In Follow Through, the U.S. Office of Education established different early childhood programs throughout the country with a view to determining which particular approach was best for children from poor families. More than twenty different childhood programs were developed and implemented in different sites around the country. About a dozen programs were compared in the final evaluation. Several cohorts of children were followed over four years of these programs, and the achievement test results were compared, mostly in contrast to a comparison site established for each experimental site. The same achievement tests were used on all sites as covariates and outcome measures. The evaluators encountered many technical problems but finally produced a comparative ranking of Follow Through programs, based on test outcomes.

Perhaps the most striking thing about the results was that the variance within programs was about as great as the variance across programs, thus making the ranking of programs questionable. That is, a particular program would have several sites; at some of these sites, the program would score well; at others, badly. Consistency of performance across sites was lacking. For this reason primarily, the data analysts said comparisons of programs could not be made. Having invested so much over such a long period of time, the Office of Education insisted in believing that a ranking of programs was possible (House, Glass, McLean, and Walker, 1978).

The injustice resides in the fact that the interests of large segments of poor students were not properly served by these findings. In fact, if a poor school district wanted to adopt the best Follow Through program, the district would be misled by the evaluation results. For reasons such as these, Cronbach (1983) advised school administrators interested in adopting such programs to examine the details of evaluation studies to find the sites that most closely matched their own district and to give attention to those results. Put another way, the same programs did not produce the same results at different sites, in spite of massive investment in development and control of these programs.

The second example is that of the evaluation of Jesse Jackson's PUSH/Excel program. Eleanor Farrar and I have written extensively about this elsewhere (Farrar and House, 1983; House, 1988). Again, PUSH/Excel was to be established on several sites around the country. This time the evaluators worked out an elaborate scheme for describing and analyzing the program itself. The program was conceived as being analyzable into separate components, which could then be assessed across sites. Considerable effort was spent documenting activities of each site. By taking the criticisms of the program from the evaluation reports, we constructed the evaluators' ideal of what the PUSH/Excel program should be: The program should be a coordinated, sequential set of standard activities, with each activity tied to specific outcomes and each activity repeated and sustained. The program had to be specified by detailed, step-by-step concrete procedures and justified by an explicit strategy and rationale. Moreover, it had to be guided and monitored by a central authority that would provide a how-to manual for participants.

PUSH/Excel was nothing like this, and when the evaluators searched for standardization across sites, they could not find it. Instead, they found different activities at different sites. From this variation the evaluators concluded that PUSH/Excel did not exist as a program. In the evaluators' judgment, there was no program. A program had to have standard components, and PUSH/Excel had none. Participants at different sites conducted different activities, local initiative being one of Jackson's original ideas. Drawing on the conclusions of this evaluation, newspaper headlines declared that Jackson had taken federal money but had not developed a program. The injustice here is striking: The results of the evaluation helped eliminate an educational program for poor black youths in the inner cities and were used in ensuing presidential campaigns as evidence that Jackson could not manage large enterprises. The evaluators conscientiously applied an elaborate evaluation model that had been developed in evaluating rural development projects in Thailand and that included qualitative data collection, including interviews with students and parents. The conclusions drawn were predetermined by the presumptions of the evaluation model used.

Here we have two different evaluations, one heavily quantitative and having a complex experimental design and the other significantly qualitative and having a simple pretest/posttest design. Both evaluations resulted in serious injustices that were damaging to the interests of impoverished people. The key element in both cases was the way variations in programs and outcomes were interpreted by the evaluators. The injustices of both evaluations derive from two sources: our particular conception of causation and the way the programs were defined. Both of these elements are closely connected and deeply embedded within evaluation's conceptual structure.

## Causation and Methods

Let us consider a classic statement of causation in evaluation from Suchman's *Evaluative Research* (1967): "The most identifying feature of evaluative research is the presence of some goal or objective whose measure of attainment constitutes the main focus of the research problem. . . . Characterized this way, one may formulate an evaluation project in terms of a series of hypotheses which state the 'Activities A, B, C will produce results X, Y, and Z' " (pp. 37–38). This formulation, or something similar, is repeated in much of evaluation literature.

Both the Follow Through and PUSH/Excel evaluations subscribed to this notion of cause and effect. In the Follow Through evaluation, it was expected that programs at different sites would produce similar results. But, in fact, this was not the case. In the PUSH/Excel evaluation, evaluators expected that the program would have the same components at all sites and that those components would produce the same results. For example, students signing the pledge to join the local PUSH/Excel program were expected to have one of only a few alternative experiences prespecified by the evaluators, and these experiences would lead to pre-specified outcomes. The evaluators expected to be able to determine exactly the outcome of signing the pledge across all sites and thereby identify the effectiveness of that particular component. Hence, the program would be built surely and slowly of precise components and their corresponding outcomes.

The analogy in both cases is to engineering; that is, a particular program construction could and would produce a certain outcome, just as one might construct a television set by matching components. In other words, the expectation was that activity A, the program, would be followed by activity B, the outcome. Along with this conception of causation there is the corresponding notion that the program consists of engineered components for which one can specify exact outcomes. Social programs are conceived of as machines, assembly lines, and pipelines—industrial metaphors that convey standardized components and totally predictable outcomes. Loosely connected activities or local programs derived from nonstandard sources appear not to be programs at all, according to these conceptions. Thus a particular definition of a program is implied by the overall conception of it. The way a program is defined is therefore a major methodology issue.

In a world of highly regular events, where "Activities A, B, C will produce results X, Y, and Z," formal experimentation makes good sense. According to Suchman (1967), "The ideal evaluation study would follow the classic experimental model. . . . This model represents the ideal experimental design from which all adaptations must be derived. . . . The basic logic of proof and verification will be traceable to this model" (p. 93, 102). The best evaluation design is the pretest/posttest control group: "The logic of this design is foolproof. Ideally, there is no element of fallibility. Whatever differences are observed between the experimental and control groups, once the above conditions are satisfied, must be attributable to the program being evaluated" (pp. 95–96).

According to Cook and Campbell (1979), one can determine which activities cause precisely which events by employing the methods of inductive logic developed by John Stuart Mill. "Mill's most significant contribution—for causal analysis purposes—consists of his work on the methods of agreement, differences, and concomitant variation. . . . The Method of Agreement states that an effect will be present when the cause is present; the Method of Difference states that the effect will be absent when the cause is absent; and the Method of Concomitant Variation implies that when both of the above relationships are observed, causal inference will be all the stronger since certain other interpretations of the covariation between the cause and effect can be ruled out" (p. 18). As Mill (1974 [1843]) put it, "The backward state of the Moral Sciences can only be remedied by applying to them the methods of Physical Science, duly extended and generalized. . . . It is by generalizing the methods successfully . . . that we may hope to remove this blot on the face of science" (pp. 833–834).

Both the substance and moral fervor of this message were championed in the formative days of evaluation. As Campbell (1969) stated, "[Quasi-experiments and true experiments] . . . stand together in contrast with a morass of obfuscation and self-deception. . . . We must provide political stances that permit true experiments, or good quasi-experiments" (p. 428). Seminal works, such as that of Campbell and Stanley (1962), presented the basic methodology: "This chapter is committed to the experiment: as the only means for settling disputes regarding educational practice, as the only way of verifying educational improvements, and as the only way of establishing a cumulative tradition in which improvements can be introduced without the danger of a faddish discard of old wisdom in favor of inferior novelties" (p. 171).

These ideas were carried out in the formation of federal policies by government officials such as Alice Rivlin, former assistant secretary of the Department of Health, Education, and Welfare and director of the Congressional Budget Office. "In other words, the conditions of scientific experiments should be realized as nearly as possible. . . . Individual project leaders have to agree to follow the plan and to use common measures of what is done and what is accomplished so that the results can be compared. . . . Information necessary to improve the effectiveness of social services is impossible to obtain any other way. . . . Effective functioning of the system depends on measures of achievement" (Rivlin, 1971, pp. 91, 108, 140).

Experimental and quasi-experimental designs, such as that of the Follow Through program, became the preferred methods of evaluation. The PUSH/Excel evaluation employed a simple pretest/posttest design and qualitative methods. Underlying both these evaluations, however, is a particular conception of causation, variously called the Humean conception of causation or the regularity theory of causation, that is fundamentally incorrect.

This conception is incorrect in that reality is construed too simply. In Cronbach's (1983) terminology, there are too many interactions. "Interactions are ubiquitous—that is the 'Achilles heel' of the behavioral sciences" (p. 150). In contrast to a standard view of causation, such as Suchman's, and following Mackie's (1974) analysis of causation, Cronbach formulates a causal law this way: "In S, all (ABC or DEF or JKL) are followed by P," (p. 139), where the letters refer to events or situations or to the absence of some objects or events. However, ABC may be sufficient, but not necessary, for P to occur, because P may just as likely be preceded by DEF or JKL. In other words, P may occur without ABC. On the other hand, ABC is sufficient for P to occur if all elements—A, B, and C—occur together but not if only AB or AC or BC occur.

The situation may be even more complex, as Mackie's (1974) original formulation of causal regularities demonstrates: "All F (A . . . B . . . or D . . . H . . . or . . . ) are P" (p. 66), where the ellipses indicate missing events or conditions that affect the outcome P but that are not represented in the law and about which we know little. Such elliptical, or "gappy," propositions represent the true state of our knowledge of social causation better than statements of simple regularity, according to Mackie and Cronbach.

The problem the standard formulation of causation poses for the evaluator is that if event A is the treatment or program, the program is neither necessary nor sufficient for effect P to occur. The program is only part of a larger array of events that may be followed by P. Furthermore, we are ignorant of what many of these events are, as Mackie represents by the ellipses. Hence, specifying the treatment in an experimental design may actually be misleading, because it may lead one to believe that program A is either necessary or sufficient for the outcome to occur when, in actuality, it is not. In other words, an experiment cannot provide a critical test for the effectiveness of a program. Traditional experimental design often mistakes the program or treatment for a sufficient condition, one that will produce the outcome by itself, when in reality the program is an "inus" (insufficient but nonredundant part of an unnecessary but sufficient) condition.

In a world in which "activities A, B, C will produce results X, Y, and Z," the program may be a sufficient cause and the experiment a critical test of its efficacy. However, such is not the world of social programs. The variability experienced in the Follow Through evaluation reflects the fact that activities A, B, C produced quite different results, depending on many factors. PUSH/Excel, a set of related but loosely integrated activities, was successful in Chattanooga, where certain other factors were operative, such as a determined political power structure, black teachers, southern black students, and strong local advocates, but the program did not succeed in several other settings. The evaluators interpreted the lack of standardized components as proof that there was no program at all, a direct inference from the evaluators' own explicit notion of program and implicit conception of causation. They were misled by their underlying assumptions.

## Program Definition

The Humean, or regularity, theory conceives causation as regular contingent relations among events that one can predict with some degree of probability. Thus the relationship between the program and its outcomes is construed as a relationship between two contingent events, even though one may not know what the program event actually consisted of. Only the presence or absence of the program event and the presence or absence of the outcome event is necessary for evaluating the success of the program. After all, one can comparatively evaluate two stereo systems without understanding the nature of their components. But physical analogies are misleading here in the sense that a machine can be separated from its environment in a way that a social program cannot.

Social programs are complex composites produced by many factors that interact to produce variable outcomes. Determining contingent relations between the program and its outcomes is not as simple as the regularity theory posits. As Manicas and Secord (1983) point out, "Events are the conjunctures of structured processes and are always the outcome of complex causal configurations at the same and at many different levels. If this is the case, then we can also say that causal processes may have surprising effects. They need not, for example, yield the outcomes they usually do" (p. 399).

A program is not a machine with a simple determined outcome, as physical analogies imply, but rather an event caused by several factors. An event such as a cocktail party has a recognizable form but may take different directions depending on the factors that produce it. A cocktail party will not turn out exactly the same way each time, even if one invites the same people and makes the same preparations. Teaching a class is also an event. One can teach the same course exactly the same way, using the same books, and yet it will turn out differently each time. The expert teacher does not standardize her routines, expecting to produce the same results but, on the contrary, develops a repertoire of skills, techniques, and ideas that enable her to respond and adjust to different situations and still produce superior educational results. Understanding such events requires a different conception of causation than that of the standard regularity theory.

How the program is defined seriously affects the evaluation and deserves to be a subject of serious study. For example, whether the program is conceived metaphorically as a machine or as an assembly line affects the evaluation because criteria appropriate to those domains are applied to the program itself. In much of the evaluation literature, program invariability is either taken for granted, as in Campbell and Stanley (1962) where the program is simply an "X," or variability is treated as a source of error, as in Cook and Campbell (1979) where one is urged to ". . . make the treatment and its implementation as standard as possible across occasions of implementation" (p. 43).

As noted before, how a program is defined affects its evaluation. More attention recently has been paid to this definition. Qualitative evaluators have made program description a major focus of their efforts, and those within the experimental tradition have begun considering the problem as well (Bickman, 1987; Shadish, 1987). For example, Chen and Rossi

(1984) argue against the "black box" approach to program definition, which has dominated the experimental literature, and advocate program specification based on social science theory. "We have argued for a paradigm that accepts experiments and quasi experiments as dominant research designs, but that emphasizes that these devices should be used in conjunction with a priori knowledge and theory to build models of the treatment process and implementation system" (p. 354). Whether social science theory is equal to the task remains to be seen, but at least the problem is recognized.

Program specification based on social science theory is not what we have had. There is not much scientific about the PUSH/Excel program specification, although it is based on a type of means/ends rationality. Program definition derives from a number of sources and methods, and McClintock (1987) has provided a useful summary of these "conceptual heuristics," which include metaphors, causal modeling, and concept maps. Program definition is an area worthy of further attention.

All this is not to say that experiments or quasi experiments cannot be useful methods of program evaluation. The point is that results must be interpreted more carefully and equivocally than in the past and that expectations as to what these methods might accomplish should be more modest. They are not the foolproof guides that Suchman envisioned. Methods are no substitute for matters of substance. The social world is far more complex than we have supposed, and a major source of error resides in our standard conception of causation, which is inadequate. We need to abandon the Humean/regularity theory and move on to more correct conceptions.

## Injustice and Method

How do these methodological problems contribute to injustices? If these methods apply to all programs evaluated and errors are randomly distributed across populations, then these errors are simply errors of method, not injustices. If injustices exist, it must be that the interests of certain groups of people are being systematically abused somehow, as in the case of craniometry.

From the craniometry example I drew two conclusions: First, the complexity and precision of research methods is no guarantee of their impartiality. Second, the intellectual and ideological climate of the age can seriously affect how studies are conducted and what conclusions are drawn, in spite of objective methodology. The nineteenth-century ideological context was such that scientists believed women and other races to be less intelligent than white males, and elaborate objective methods were developed to support these beliefs. What was the intellectual climate that prevailed when the contemporary practice of evaluation developed?

After World War II, the United States reached an unprecedented pinnacle of power, influence, and wealth and became a model to be emulated for much of the world. Americans were united in what Hodgson (1978, p. 76) calls the "ideology of the liberal consensus," which includes the following beliefs:

• The American free enterprise system creates abundance for all. It has a revolutionary potential for social justice.
• Ever-increasing economic growth makes it possible to meet people's needs so that conflict between classes is obsolete.
• There is a natural harmony of interests in society. American society is becoming more equal and is on the verge of abolishing social classes.
• Social problems can be solved like industrial problems: The problem is first identified; programs are designed to solve it by government enlightened by social science; money and other resources are applied; the problems will be solved.
• The main threat to this beneficent system comes from the deluded adherents of Marxism.
• It is the duty of the United States to bring the benefits of this free enterprise system to the rest of the world.

These beliefs constituted the ideological background from which early evaluation emerged. It was believed that social problems such as poverty and racism could be solved within the framework of American society and that nothing was wrong with the framework itself. Social engineering, guided by social science and freed from politics and popular superstition, could eliminate the ugly remnants of a less enlightened age. Only will and resources were needed. Put another way, certain activities would produce certain outcomes and solve certain problems. How did these beliefs affect whose interests were served or not served?

First, the programs we evaluate are not randomly drawn from all programs but tend to be programs for the poor and disadvantaged. Follow Through is a program for poor and disadvantaged in grades K through 3. PUSH/Excel was a program for black teenagers in the inner cities. Income maintenance, drug abuse, juvenile crime prevention, and a multitude of other programs are typically for poor people. Evaluation as a government mandate began in 1965, when Robert Kennedy attached a rider to the Title I Elementary and Secondary Education Act to ensure that the interests of poor black students and parents would be served. Thus our methodology errors differentially affect the welfare of the poor and dispossessed.

Though it is true that evaluation has been extended to a great number of programs not intended to serve the poor and powerless, it is also true that recipients of program benefits are almost always in a less powerful position than program providers and evaluators. Hence, there is differential power within every program. The possibility of some injustice exists even when recipients are teachers, patients, or other people we do not think of as being disadvantaged. This injustice problem is compounded when the recipient group is socially disadvantaged.

Second, our criteria of merit are often differentially applied across programs. Consider the criteria for success in the PUSH/Excel evaluation: A coherent program should be a coordinated, sequential set of standard activities, with each activity tied to specific outcomes and each activity repeated and sustained. The program has to be specified by detailed, step-by-step, concrete procedures and justified by an explicit strategy and rationale. Moreover, it has to be guided and monitored by a central authority that provides a how-to manual for participants. These criteria are inappropriate for defining what a program must be. What if these criteria were applied rigorously to university programs? It is likely that not one university department in the country could stand up to such an examination. Such inappropriate criteria are rarely applied to universities, but when they are, professors become rightfully indignant.

One is reminded again of how Broca and the nineteenth-century craniometricians applied their inappropriate criteria differentially to arrive at their infamous findings, making exceptions for small-brained Frenchmen but not for women. If our evaluation methodology employs inappropriate criteria, it has differential effects because it is most often applied to programs for the poor and powerless. Hence, we are in the realm of injustice. Of course, we must also remember the reverse side: When we are correct, we are pursuing social justice because evaluation is a democratizing institution, or at least should be. Evaluators should try to represent the interests of the poor and powerless, just as the interests of other groups are already represented.

Third, there is the distinct possibility that our methodology systematically misguides us as to what is wrong with programs. When these programs are judged to be failures, what is blamed is poor conceptualization and planning on the part of the developers, traits of individual participants and recipients, poor implementation, politics, ambiguous goal statements, unrealistic expectations, lack of coordination, inadequate training, and a host of other contingencies. The societal framework itself is rarely faulted. Generally, the program is blamed for failure rather than factors in the social structure, such as social class or economic structures or gender-reproducing mechanisms. The background ideology itself constrains other available explanations and potential solutions.

Finally, there remains the question of whether the Humean (or regularity) conception of causation systematically works against the interests of various groups of people. This is a very complex question, but it seems that this conception is at fault, at least in the way it has been employed. The Humean conception implies that experts using the proper methods can ascertain the best programs and approaches for addressing social ills. This attitude delegitimizes knowledge derived from other sources and people, leading to a form of scientism: Only information derived from certain techniques is true knowledge. In reality, information gathered from other sources, from participants, for example, is critical to a full understanding of social processes. This is not to deny the role of experts in addressing social ills but rather to point out that experts do not have exclusive knowledge of those ills.

These beliefs, along with our heritage of academic ideas such as the Humean conception of causation, constituted the intellectual climate in which the contemporary methodology of evaluation developed, from which have emerged some systematic injustices. These injustices are often subtle and unintentional perhaps, but they are real nonetheless. To correct them, we must revise our conception of evaluation, which is no longer adequate for the world in which we now live.

## References

Bickman, L. (ed.). *Using Program Theory in Evaluation.* New Directions for Program Evaluation, no. 33. San Francisco: Jossey-Bass, 1987.

Campbell, D. T. "Reforms as Experiments." *American Psychologist,* 1969, *24,* 409–429.

Campbell, D. T., and Stanley, J. C. "Experimental and Quasi-Experimental Designs for Research on Teaching." In N. L. Gage (ed.), *Handbook of Research on Teaching.* Skokie, Ill.: Rand McNally, 1962.

Chen, H. T., and Rossi, P. H. "Evaluating with Sense: The Theory Driven Approach." In R. F. Conner (ed.), *Evaluation Studies Review Annual,* no. 9. Newbury Park, Calif.: Sage, 1984.

Cook, T. D., and Campbell, D. T. *Quasi-Experimentation: Design and Analysis Issues for Field Studies.* Boston: Houghton Mifflin, 1979.

Cronbach, L. J. *Designing Evaluations of Educational and Social Programs.* San Francisco: Jossey-Bass, 1983.

Farrar, E., and House, E. R. "The Evaluation of PUSH/Excel: A Case Study." In A. Bryk (ed.), *Stakeholder-Based Evaluation.* New Directions for Program Evaluation, no. 17. San Francisco: Jossey-Bass, 1983.

Gould, S. J. *The Mismeasure of Man.* New York: Norton, 1981.

Hodgson, G. *America in Our Time.* New York: Vintage, 1978.

House, E. R. *Jesse Jackson and the Politics of Charisma: The Rise and Fall of the PUSH/Excel Program,* Boulder, Colo.: Westview Press, 1988.

House, E. R. "Evaluation and Social Justice: Where Are We?" In M. W. McLaughlin and D. C. Phillips (eds.), *Evaluation and Education at Quarter Century.* Chicago: University of Chicago Press, in press.

House, E. R., Glass, G. V., McLean, L., and Walker, D. "No Simple Answer: A Critique of the Follow Through Evaluation." *Harvard Educational Review,* 1978, *48,* 128–160.

McClintock, C. "Conceptual and Action Heuristics: Tools for the Evaluator." In L. Bickman (ed.), *Using Program Theory in Evaluation.* New Directions for Program Evaluation, no. 33. San Francisco: Jossey-Bass, 1987.

Mackie, J. L. *The Cement of the Universe: A Study of Causation.* Oxford, England: Oxford University Press, 1974.

Manicas, P. T., and Secord, P. F. "Implications for Psychology of the New Philosophy of Science." *American Psychologist,* 1983, *38,* 399–413.

Mill, J. S. *A System of Logic: Ratiocinative and Inductive.* Toronto, Canada: University of Toronto Press, 1974. (Originally published 1843.)

Rivlin, A. M. *Systematic Thinking for Social Action.* Washington, D.C.: Brookings Institution, 1971.

Shadish, W. R., Jr. "Program Micro- and Macrotheories: A Guide for Social Change." In L. Bickman (ed.), *Using Program Theory in Evaluation.* New Directions for Program Evaluation, no. 33. San Francisco: Jossey-Bass, 1987.

Suchman, E. A. *Evaluative Research.* New York: Russell Sage Foundation, 1967.

*Ernest R. House is director of the Laboratory for Policy Studies, School of Education, University of Colorado, Boulder. His latest book is* Jesse Jackson and the Politics of Charisma: The Rise and Fall of the PUSH/Excel Program *(1988).*

*Values, beliefs, and human interests are embedded in evaluation theory and practice. For organizations such as public schools to engage seriously in improvement and change efforts, this normative content must be explicitly addressed. Critical inquiry provides an evaluative paradigm for doing so.*

# Evaluation as Critical Inquiry: School Improvement as a Case in Point

*Kenneth A. Sirotnik, Jeannie Oakes*

There have been many new directions in the theory and practice of evaluation over the past quarter of a century or more. During this time program evaluation has emerged as a body of knowledge in its own right. Beginning with the tradition of evaluation research (Suchman, 1967), just a sampling of the many subsequent directions includes discrepancy evaluation (Provus, 1971), decision-oriented evaluation (Stufflebeam and others, 1971), goal-free evaluation (Scriven, 1972b), adversary evaluation (Owens, 1973), transactional evaluation (Rippey, 1973), responsive evaluation (Stake, 1975), democratic evaluation (MacDonald, 1976), illuminative evaluation (Parlett and Hamilton, 1976), evaluation as connoisseurship (Eisner, 1977), utilization-focused evaluation (Patton, 1978), qualitative evaluation (Patton, 1980), benefit-cost evaluation (Thompson, 1980), effective evaluation (Guba and Lincoln, 1981), stakeholder-based evaluation (Bryk, 1983), and naturalistic evaluation (Williams, 1986).

Although many of these directions differ in philosophical underpinnings and proposed methodologies, they share one crucial feature. They advocate no value position—that is, no moral imperative, no ethical commitment, no normative stance serves to make explicit what "good" is at the heart of the evaluative inquiry. Most of the evaluation models we have seen have, in effect, either refused to consider the issue of values by claiming them to be metaphysical concerns and not amenable to scientific, objective study. Or they have taken a subjectivist-relativist position—one that acknowledges the presence and importance of values but

NEW DIRECTIONS FOR PROGRAM EVALUATION, no. 45, Spring 1990 © Jossey-Bass Inc., Publishers sees them as relevant only as they are interpreted or negotiated, or both, within specific contexts of human understanding and social interaction.

In fact, inquiry is not value free. There are some values that we cannot negotiate away no matter what the evaluative problem or setting might be. Moreover, there may well be some values that we wish to hold at the heart of evaluative inquiry to use as a standard for interpreting whatever empirical data might emerge. As the title and thematic thrust of this volume suggests, social justice may be one of these values. In fact, it may be necessary to build an evaluative philosophy and practice on the belief in, and valuing of, social justice.

We do not intend to elaborate on the notion of social justice here; other contributors are doing that, and a number of interesting expositions have appeared elsewhere (for example, Ackerman, 1980; Dworkin, 1977; Gewirth, 1978; Phillips, 1986; Rawls, 1971, 1985). We will simply note that the conception of social justice that we have in mind is not merito-cratic (a privilege for some); rather it is democratic (a birthright for all). Social justice is not based on maximizing average benefits, where some persons can gain at the expense of others, but rather reflects something as simple and universal as the Golden Rule (Do unto others as you would have them do unto you) and its obverse (Do not do unto others as you would not have them do unto you). Without debating the details, this is close, in essence, to Rawls's (1971) theory of justice as fairness. If we take seriously the notion of liberty and justice for all, we should find it much less appealing—in fact, we would find it intolerable—to base evaluative inquiry on ethical stances rooted in racial determinism, hedon-ism, nihilism, and the like, or on no ethical stance whatsoever. We can think of no more fundamentally American point of departure into inquir-ies of human affairs than one based on social justice.

Kohlberg's (1971) analysis of moral development stages is relevant here insofar as the ethics of social justice compose the philosophical orientation of his sixth and highest level of moral development. Of par-ticular interest is his response to critics (such as Alston, 1971), who voiced classic relativistic arguments that *any* value could be as logically prescriptive as the principle of justice. As Kohlberg (1971, pp. 221-222) states:

> The fact that psychological study shows that no one does use unjust "principles" in a formally principled way is no proof that they cannot. However, it is of more moment that no philosopher ever has seriously attempted to demonstrate that an alternative substantive principle to justice could function in a universal prescriptive fashion in a satisfac-tory way. Alston is correct in saying that I have not proved that justice is the only possibility, but he neglects to point out that no one has successfully argued for an alternative.

Social justice as considered here also forms the core of a corpus of work in the reconstruction of social and political theory, a large part of which can be generally referred to as critical theory (see Geuss, 1981). This work provides the epistemological connections between critical theory and evaluation. To be specific, if one accepts the proposition that inquiry is never value free and accepts social justice as the ethical starting and ending points for moral argument, then the accumulated body of work by such authors as Bernstein (1978), Freire (1973), Habermas (1971, 1979), Horkheimer (1972), and many others points the way toward a useful epistemological synthesis—one that we have called critical inquiry (Oakes, 1986; Sirotnik and Oakes, 1983, 1986)—that is evaluative by its very nature.

Although we think it can be argued that this perspective on evaluation is generic to any sustained inquiry in the social sciences, we feel it is important to situate the argument in a specific context—namely, the one with which we are most familiar: public schooling. Doing so, we join a number of writers who have attempted to reconstruct the idea of evaluation from a more critical perspective, for example, Berlak and Berlak (1981), Carr and Kemmis (1986), and Coomer (1981), to name just a few.

In this chapter, our previous work on critical inquiry will be summarized and extended as an evaluative process for school improvement and renewal. We do this by first developing a thumbnail sketch of a critical analysis of the current state of public schooling in America. Second, we outline the paradigm shift required to develop the idea of critical inquiry. Third, we begin a discussion of methods, issues, and concerns around what it might mean to do critical inquiry in schools. Here, it will become clear that we are not dealing with program evaluation in the usual sense of a specific intervention to be described and appraised. Nor are we dealing with evaluators as outside experts who come in to do appraisals. Rather, the program in our example is schooling itself; the evaluators are the educators themselves, although certainly external collaborators may be involved as well.

## Schooling in America

After spending a quarter of a century and billions of dollars on school improvement efforts, the gaps between what educators intend to do, what the public expects to have happen in schools, and what actually goes on in them seem to grow increasingly wider. And the period between cycles of dissatisfaction and flurries of reform rhetoric seems to be growing shorter. The criticisms and exhortations of the 1980s may go down in history as the most sustained of these cycles. As Goodlad (1981) noted at the beginning of the decade, however, there has been a qualitative difference between yesterday's and today's attacks: "Yesterday, the attacks usually were against the people who ran the schools—their wrongheadedness or their mindlessness—but rarely against the institution. Today, as often as not, the attacks are against the institution itself, not just those who run it." (p. 1). To put it another way, Silberman's (1970) "crisis of the classroom" has become a full-blown crisis of schooling. Why?

## A Critical View

Historically, the stated goals for schools, supported by the public, have included four broad areas: (1) acquisition of fundamental academic knowledge and skills, (2) preparation for productive work and responsible participation in economic life, (3) development of skills and understanding requisite for active participation in the complex social and political structures of society, and (4) personal development toward fulfillment (Goodlad, 1984). Yet the gaps between these intents and actual school practice can be readily inferred from studies of classroom practices from the turn of the century to the present (Goodlad, 1984; Oakes, 1985; Powell, Farrar, and Cohen, 1985; Sizer, 1984; Sirotnik, 1983). Further, the fact that the loftiest of our educational aims—developing all individuals as literate, culturally enlightened, critical thinkers who will create a just and democratic society—is rarely articulated provides additional evidence of an institution off course or, at minimum, acritical about its own purposes and practices.

But the problem is larger than schooling itself. The complex cultural phenomena we call schools have evolved to their present forms as adaptations to a socio-political context that is largely incompatible with the best of our educational intents. Another set of goals—usually unspoken ones—place schools in a central role in maintaining society in its current forms. When we acknowledge this implicit set of goals, schools' resistance to reform becomes more easily understood. Goals that direct schools to maintain the status quo often run counter to innovations directed at the full development of all individuals. The creation of a literate, culturally enlightened, critically thinking citizenry might very well wreak havoc with our current political, social, and economic structures.

Philosophers and educators have debated for centuries the extent to which education should develop the individual or serve the needs of the state. The conflict continues because the ideal just and democratic state—one that is best served by fully educated individuals—has yet to be developed. The usual tenuous compromise or resolution of this conflict is that individual development proceeds only to the point where it begins to threaten the status quo.

A major barrier, then, to reforms that attempt to bridge the gap between educational intents and school practice is that they run headlong into a set of beliefs and assumptions that permeate society and dictate how schools should operate in order to maintain society as it is. While this is not a consciously mapped-out conspiracy, this socio-political phenomenon has the consequence of perpetuating schooling norms that run counter to the best-intentioned goals of education. And the problem is greatly exacerbated by an uncritical acceptance of these norms. That is, we usually think of schools as neutral, nonpolitical places that educate children as well as they can. We assume that schools are eager for practices that will enable them to do better. Change attempts usually take these assumptions for granted and, as a result, concentrate their energies on developing better educational technologies. Little attention is given to the values and beliefs on which school practice rests.

While more and better educational technology is required for school change, consideration of normative (as well as technical) questions needs to become a serious and rigorous part of ongoing evaluation efforts. This, of course, is antithetical to homeostatic mechanisms that schools and school systems have developed. It is little wonder, then, that school innovations have achieved little in the way of lasting successes. Sociologists and anthropologists who have studied schools intensively could probably have predicted this result. But perhaps it has been necessary to accumulate years of experience to verify this outcome and raise the consciousness of the research and evaluation community to new paradigms of inquiry and action.

## A Cultural View

One of the most powerful forces influencing how a school conducts itself is the culture that has developed there. The notion of the school as a culture has been variously discussed, not only by anthropologists (Henry, 1971; Spindler, 1955; and Wolcott, 1973, to name only a few) but by others from a variety of disciplines (for example, Barker and Gump, 1964; Goodlad, 1975; Jackson, 1968; Lortie, 1975; Sarason, 1982; and Waller, 1932).

While definitions of culture vary, they generally include the notion that culture comprises the solutions that groups of people derive for the problems they face. Culture, then, is purposeful in embodying the roles, norms, and expectations people develop as they try to make sense of their environment. The particular solutions that a group chooses determine the organizational structures, patterns of behavior, and ways of interrelating that constitute a way of life that has meaning for that group. These solutions also include the assumptions and beliefs that those in the setting hold about the nature of their environment and the people in it. Culture, therefore, is more than simply a group's ways of doing things; it is also the meanings the group attaches to these approaches. Furthermore, all of these elements—organizational structures, behavior patterns, underlying beliefs, and meanings—have both manifest and latent consequences for the members of the group and the events that take place in the setting.

This definition of culture provides a useful perspective on schools when thinking about evaluative activities. First, it leads us to see the organizational arrangements and activities of the school as purposeful; they "make sense" in the context. Even those not easily justified can be understood. Second, a cultural view demands that the school environment be approached as a whole—taking into account the interrelatedness of organizational structures, individual behaviors, and underlying beliefs— rather than as a collection of isolated or independent elements. Third, by forcing us to consider underlying assumptions and belief systems as well as observable structures and behaviors, we cannot simply describe school processes and outcomes; we must also explore why particular organizational and behavioral alternatives evolved as appropriate in a particular setting. Fourth, by directing our attention to the latent as well as manifest consequences of events in the school setting, we must broaden our definition of the outcomes of schooling and the effects of change. Taken together, elements of this cultural view of schooling compel us to approach evaluation with a sense of the wholeness and integrity of schools and permit us to consider both the sources of resistance to change and the broadest range of effects that change might have.

The local school is the setting where social, political, and historical forces affecting schooling are translated into practice; at each school this translation is likely to happen in different ways. Evaluation based only on an understanding of a more general school culture, and not on its particular form at the local school, will ignore what is most critical—the peculiar structures, behaviors, meanings, and belief systems that have evolved at that particular school. These characteristics—what Sarason (1982) calls regularities—are both the local manifestations of the general schooling culture and the school's accommodations to the social and political pressures exerted by its particular community. These local school regularities must be understood if school improvement is to be achieved, and they must also be the focus of change if improvements are to be more than trivial.

But it is exactly these regularities that are overlooked in most evaluation and improvement efforts. This oversight probably results from a belief that regularities are natural. Based on assumptions that are rarely made explicit, school regularities are seldom recognized and alternatives to them rarely conceived. Further, as Sarason (1982, p. 109) so clearly states:

> But here one runs smack into the obstacle of another characteristic of school culture: there are no vehicles of discussion, communication or

observation that allow for . . . variation to be raised and productively used for purposes of help and change.

Evaluating and improving schools requires breaking through this "natural order" of things. The question is how. In the following sections we explore the idea that the expanded methodological perspective of critical inquiry can provide the vehicles Sarason refers to and facilitate the institutionalization of school change and renewal.

## Three Faces of Inquiry

Most educational researchers and evaluators have been schooled in the tradition of the scientific method and the hypothetico-deductive paradigm, presumably borrowed from the physical sciences (Kerlinger's 1986 presentation is illustrative). Although we often stretch and shape this traditional scientific paradigm to meet the exigencies of social and behavioral research, we still think about the act of inquiry in much the same way as a physicist would in attempting to support or reject a theory of motion, light, heat, and so on. This approach derives from those schools of philosophical thought labeled variously as logical positivism, empirical analytic science, scientific empiricism, and so on.

But there are at least two other separate and general orientations for systematic inquiry having strong philosophical roots and demonstrable utility for the social sciences. The more familiar is the whole class of naturalistic methodologies. The debate between the naturalistic versus scientific modes of inquiry, of course, is an old one and is often characterized by superficial distinctions between qualitative versus quantitative or subjective versus objective methodologies. As has been argued by others (for example, Scriven, 1972a; Rist, 1977), these can be simplistic dichotomies that without proper qualification serve only to stereotype otherwise profound differences and similarities.

Although there are certainly notable differences in the array of naturalistic methodologies (for example, phenomenology, symbolic interaction, and ethnomethodology), these are all essentially oriented toward interpreting and understanding social events in terms of the meaning for the participants in those events. The emphasis on interpretation has led to the use of hermeneutics as another related model of inquiry that places a premium on interpretive understanding in contrast to the positivist tradition that focuses on explanation via prediction (see, for example, Ericson and Ellett, 1982; Ricoeur, 1981; Taylor, 1977; and Van Manen, 1975).

The second major departure from the empirical analytical tradition is less well known and much more separable—namely, the critique of knowledge. Its roots are also in the hermeneutical tradition. But as a philosophy of inquiry, it represents a significant extention of interpretive inquiry. Such critique represents the application of dialectical reason to the explanations and understandings gained through predictive and interpretive inquiries. Inquiry does not happen in a normative vacuum, as many traditional social scientists would have us believe. By definition, at the heart of dialectical reason is the search for truth through unrestrained discourse. When applied to social inquiry, the political implications can be summed up in a word: justice. A social scientist who is committed to the critique of social knowledge is, therefore, committed to the pursuit of social justice.

What, then, are the ideological stances implicit in the first two faces of inquiry? Look in any textbook in the traditional mode of empirical inquiry and you will find, in reference to the purposes of research (or science), that the aim of social science is to predict and control human behavior. Understanding is equated to empirical support of a theory. But, according to Kerlinger (1986), a theory is a "set of interrelated constructs (concepts), definitions, and propositions that represent a systematic view of phenomena by specifying relations among variables, with the purpose of explaining and predicting the phenomena" (p. 9).

Although one has to work harder to dig them out, similar frames of reference can be found in the applied forms of phenomenology. For example, Blumer (1969) defines empirical science as "an enterprise that seeks to develop images and conceptions that can successfully handle and accommodate the resistance offered by the empirical world under study" (pp. 22–23). The methodology and epistemology of symbolic interactionists are, in many respects, worlds apart from those underlying the empirical analytic tradition. But the ideas of prediction and control are inherent (if not intended) in the above quotation.

The most systematic development of the third face of inquiry has resulted in what has come to be labeled critical theory. At the core of this theory is a normative stance that eschews hegemony of any form and demands unrestrained, undominated dialogue in the process of social and political critique. It is, therefore, an epistemology of transformative action, having its roots in the traditions of Kant, Hegel, and Marx as interpreted more recently by the German philosophers Horkheimer, Adorno, Marcuse, Apel, and Habermas. But there is also a strong Latino tradition behind the idea of a critical social science, reflected primarily in the writings and practice of Paulo Freire. Moreover, an American connection can also be made in the philosophical work of John Dewey. Although it can be argued that Dewey was not a critical theorist per se, he certainly championed the idea of intellectual freedom and the democratic pursuit of knowledge through experience and action.

Habermas is among the most provocative and influential of the critical theorists. He has raised the level of consciousness of many social scientists to the essential paradigm differences underlying the three faces of inquiry. According to Habermas (1971), the epistemology and methodology underlying each of the several major traditions of inquiry is inexorably bound to fundamental and distinct human interests. (See in particular the appendix to Habermas's 1971 work.) In the interest of technical rationality, the empirical-analytic sciences predict, control, and even exploit human behavior through imposing the artificial rules of the scientific method. The naturalistic-hermeneutic sciences have a practical interest—that of understanding human behavior in a situational context, promoting some form of consensus among the participants, and perhaps even reaching some level of acceptance of what is. But a critical social science has at its core an emancipatory interest; it is not content with what is but rather with what can and should be. To this end, a critical science exposes and challenges the ideologies and human interests guiding other forms of inquiry.

To be sure, this trilogy of isomorphisms between knowledge and human interests has a good deal of seductive appeal, especially for those wishing for a strong philosophical basis for rejecting traditional science. But as we reflect on these distinctions, they become increasingly blurred, and we become increasingly sympathetic with critiques such as Bernstein's (1978, p. 43):

> It is a fiction—and not a useful methodological one—to suggest that there are categorically different types of inquiry and knowledge. But it is not a fiction—rather it is the locus of the most important controversies about the nature and limits of human knowledge, as it pertains to social and political inquiry—to see how the battle of competing technical, practical, and emancipatory cognitive interests continues to rage.

To put it another way, we suspect an epistemological trap can be created through assuming necessary and sufficient connections between method and the political content of cognitive interests. Conducting empirical analytic inquiry, for example, does not necessarily imply a hidden agenda of domination. On the other hand, a hidden agenda of domination cannot in principle survive an inquiry based on critical theory. And this, indeed, points the way out of the trap—a truly practical unification of the three faces of inquiry requires the self-correcting epistemological stance that is made to order in a critical perspective.

The practical feature we suggest is this: The substance for critique by critical theorists traditionally derives from existing knowledge (and the interests underlying this knowledge) accumulated through other modes of inquiry. What we wish to suggest here takes this process a small but significant step forward. We propose the deliberate accumulating of additional explanations and understandings—by people in a specific setting who wish to change that setting and who determine what additional information may be relevant to change efforts—for the express purpose of furthering evaluation in a constructive, critical fashion.

In other words, we propose an epistemologically valid basis on which we can (1) acknowledge critique as a legitimate method of inquiry, (2) acknowledge values and beliefs as an unavoidable medium through which inquiry is conducted, and (3) propose an inquiry approach driven by a critical theoretical stance that makes use of appropriate information gathered from naturalistic and empirical analytic inquiries.

How, then, is this working synthesis relevant for the evaluation of schooling? As logical empiricists we can obtain a tentative description of those features of the school context we are willing to operationalize by means of survey, questionnaire, test, structured interview, observation schedule, or any other method of data collection. We are opting, here, for a pragmatic stance based on a belief (rooted in experience) in the heuristic potential of data gathered in this fashion, as long as they are reasonably reliable and valid (according to traditional canons) and not overinterpreted under the guise of scientism. Our belief in the heuristic potential of this kind of information as the empirical data base of a school—that is, its ability to enrich the experiential basis for interpretation, understanding, and normative critique—requires an exploratory stance on data analysis and interpretation.

The payoff of the empirical-analytic perspective is the serving up of a continuing common base of explicit descriptive material that can act as a catalyst for further inquiry. Indeed, this suggests an important category of validity invariably left out of traditional expositions: the capability of information to nurture, stimulate, or otherwise provoke rigorous discourse. "Dialogical validity" would be a good expression for this kind of validity; other terms have been proposed by the few writers who have considered this issue (such as "catalytic validity," coined by Reason and Rowan, 1981).

The point is that while some of the information may already be known to all of the participants, and much of it known to some of the participants, a considerable portion of the information will be new to many of them. The discovery of apparent relationships among contextual elements can provide fresh insights to all participants about the way things are and can stimulate them to move to a deeper level of evaluative inquiry—to make public their private frames of reference.

Employing naturalistic methodology for the interpretation of phenomena provides a depth of understanding not permitted by the more positivistic methodologies. This second approach permits participants to add the texture of individual meanings to the description of the context. Going beyond the facts yielded by the data collected in the empirical-analytic mode, this approach adds a sense of the whole—how human beings within the context experience that context. In other words, this phenomenological perspective promotes an interpretive understanding of the organizational characteristics, human behaviors, and feelings that make up the school setting.

Outsiders make detailed observations of events within the setting and conduct interviews with participants (as is typically done in naturalistic research) to seek the meanings that the setting holds for its participants. More appropriate, however, for school-based evaluation and improvement efforts would be the meanings elicited by the people in the school. Participant reflection and interpretation of their schools could add new categories of information not permitted by conventional data collection processes. Such categories of information cannot be predetermined but emerge during the process of inquiry. Nonetheless, they are certain to include the valuing of the experiences under scrutiny, making judgments about the intrinsic worth of phenomena and assessing their importance in relation to other ends. Statements made during such a process should be supported by reasons. In this way, the participants' bases for making decisions (their underlying assumptions and belief systems) will be explicit and subject to scrutiny as well.

Finally, the third approach places knowledge gained about the school setting within its social and historical context. Building on the facts and the personal meanings gathered, the critical process offers methods for understanding and assessing the value of the social and political meanings of school events. Furthermore, norms for assessing these events and guiding future practice are embedded in critical methodology. Thus it provides a fundamental criterion for the direction of change and improvement. In these ways, critical inquiry makes possible a much fuller consideration of the implications of what is done in schools. Those in schools can gain insight into why particular practices came into being and how human interests are thereby served.

The methodology of critical reflection demands that participants be aware of how educational structures, content, and processes are linked to the social and political forces inside and outside the school. Such questions as "What are the effects on participants of the organized patterns in operation?" and "Who benefits from these organized patterns?" force participants to examine both the manifest and latent consequences of their own educational practices. Latent consequences necessarily include social, political, and economic, as well as purely intellectual, effects and benefits of practices. By bringing these relationships to the surface, educational practitioners can become aware that school practices and their rationale for them are not merely commonsensical, neutral, or benign but grow out of past and present circumstances that affect everyone.

During the process of critical inquiry participants become conscious of how current ways of schooling are grounded in the larger historical and social context of the culture as well as in the particular institutional and social context. Participants also become aware that the range of typical educational alternatives is limited to those reflecting the dominant social, political, and economic modes. This kind of awareness, which is not widespread in school planning and decision making, should enable those considering improvement in schools to move beyond conventional and limited thinking.

But inquiry driven by critical theory goes further than freeing participants from socially influenced and largely unquestioned assumptions, which limit the choices and actions. The basic concern of critical theory is movement toward an emancipated form of social life, or as McCarthy (1978) puts it, the "realization of a truly rational society in which men make their own history with will and consciousness" (p. xi). Critical theory carries with it an ethical stance that directs change efforts toward nonexploitive interpersonal relationships, making human beings conscious moral agents who have a central role in determining the direction of social evolution. Thus critical theory is a social theory with a practical intention—the self-emancipation of human beings from the constraints of domination in whatever form and however concealed by social, political, and economic patterns and ideologies (McCarthy, 1978).

The relevance of such a potentially emancipatory and purposeful kind of inquiry to the process of school improvement should be self-evident. Both the process and aim of critical theory are consistent with what we most often claim to be the fundamental aim of education itself— the view of cultivating the best in human beings so they may create a just society. A critical, self-reflective knowledge of both the culture of the school and the outside social and political context that shapes their decisions, actions, and rationales might enable educators to redirect the practices of schooling toward more humane means and ends.

The methodology of critique rests on competent communication and on a belief in the potential of groups to reach a justified consensus about the truth of what exists, gaining thereby a larger view of the social context and of universal human interests. In Habermas's (1979) view, if discourse were to take place under ideal conditions (which include the suspension of all motives other than the intention of coming to an understanding about what exists and the determination of the best course of action), then the force of the better argument would permit reaching a justified consensus. While this is an oversimplified description of the process of critique, the basic requirement is unlimited opportunity for discussion, free of constraints from any source. Thus the methodology of critique is inextricably tied to its aims. The ideal circumstances of life— freedom and justice—are also necessary for critical inquiry and action to occur. Because of this match, the means versus ends dichotomy is eliminated in the theory and practice of critical inquiry.

Consider the implications for schooling if this kind of critical inquiry were applied to taken-for-granted school organizational and instructional practices—for example, norm-referenced testing, curriculum tracking, or competitive classroom reward structures. If these almost universal practices were to be the focus of critical discourse, their histories and underlying assumptions would be revealed, the kind of social reality they imply would be made explicit, and their consequences for individuals and society would be uncovered. It is likely that they would be revealed to be in conflict with educators' conceptions of humane and democratic schooling. The recognition of how these practices constrain the attainment of a schooling process that serves the interests of all students might lead educators to practice a more ideal conceptualization of education. Criterion-referenced measurement, mastery learning, heterogeneous grouping, and cooperative classroom learning are just a few of the practices that might take on new value. Such procedures would become more defensible on ethical grounds, given their apparent humane consequences.

All this, of course, is speculative. Consensus about the truth of current practice and decisions about desirable alternatives can come only from those in the school setting as they engage in the process of self-reflection and critical inquiry. Moreover, such consensus is only possible if the conditions for critical discourse are established.

For school people, participation in this kind of evaluative process would mean the involvement of the school staff in communication characterized by free exploration, honest exchange, and nonmanipulative discussion of existing and deliberately generated knowledge. The focus of this discourse would be critical questions such as: What goes on in this school? Who benefits from the way things are? How might educational practice work toward liberation from exploitive relationships and the domination of current social, political, and economic interests? How can schools help develop the capacity to make free and responsible choices about the direction of individual lives and the evolution of society? The potential contribution of this third phase of inquiry to significant educational change is promising. The kind of emancipatory understanding that can come from critical reflection about the school within its social setting is necessary to build a responsive, renewing climate in schools.

## Toward Doing Critical Inquiry

Our vision of "doing" critical inquiry can be likened to wearing three hats at the same time: (1) a top hat representing critical inquiry and a dedication to explanation and understanding within a normative perspective that maintains a continued dialectic between knowledge, justice, and human interests; (2) a middle hat representing interpretive inquiry and a desire to understand the conditions of schooling in terms of historical and current school events and peoples' experiences of those events; and (3) a bottom hat representing empirical analytic inquiry and a willingness to use descriptive (survey-type), experimental, and/or quasi-experimental methods to yield information of potential value not only for pedagogical improvement but also for furthering understanding and normative critique.

Furthermore, the competent use of language in social discourse is indispensable to doing critical inquiry. By this we do not mean grammatical or syntactical competence. We are referring, rather, to ingredients necessary for sharing understanding, trust, and active engagement in the process of change. As we have discussed above, Habermas's (1979) notion of approaching an ideal situation for discourse provides the guidelines for this kind of competent communication. Together with the synthesis implied by the foregoing epistemological stance, these principles define an operating mode that must eventually come to be shared and internalized by all involved.

Yet this mode alone is insufficient to break through the barriers to change in schools. Basic issues such as content, intervention, legitimation, motivation, and individual differences are of consequence to anyone attempting to use the idea of critical inquiry as evaluation practice. Given the constraints in the social contexts of institutions, people do not generally interact with one another in the way we suggest.

The ultimate dilemma is that the very fact that a new perspective on inquiry and change is needed guarantees that barriers exist to the cultivation of this perspective—barriers that are not neatly accounted for by the canons of the perspective itself. Consider, for example, the following scenario taken from a past experience in schools (names and inconsequential details have been fictionalized).

*Case Example.* Las Montanas is a small- to medium-sized school district (two senior high, three junior high, and eleven elementary schools) located in a suburban area adjacent to a major West Coast urban center. The community residents range in economic status from the middle to the lower levels, with the median family income being approximately $15,000. Roughly half the community is of Hispanic origin, many recently immigrated from Mexico; less than 5 percent represent other minorities, and thus Anglos compose approximately 45 percent of the community.

The district is essentially centralized; the superintendent exercises a good deal of control through a highly bureaucratized organizational structure. All principals report to an assistant superintendent. Each principal is responsible for yearly school plans, which are monitored by the assistant superintendent. Over the last several years the superintendent has circulated position papers to all administrators and staff on the several principles of school effectiveness and has conducted a few inservice workshops on this topic. These were oriented around such notions as principal leadership, academic emphasis, learning expectations, discipline and control, and actively engaged learning time. Armed with this information, principals and the staff were expected to put their schools on a direct course toward excellence. In accordance with school effectiveness theory, excellence was assumed to be reflected in standardized achievement test score rankings, particularly in comparison with other schools of similar demographic composition.

Different school staffs handled this mandate in different ways. For example, at one elementary school, banners were hung with the slogans "High Expectations" and "Emphasize Academics" in the library room. Teachers also began to meet informally to attempt to figure out just what increased time on task meant and how they might recognize it in actual operation.

At Riverview Elementary School, things went a little differently. The principal and staff seemed virtually paralyzed by what appeared to them to be directionless directives. Riverview had a particularly high Hispanic enrollment of nearly two-thirds; most of the remaining students were Anglos. The ethnic composition of the staff was nearly the mirror image: three-quarters Anglo and one-quarter Hispanic (including the principal). Riverview's state achievement test scores were low, being either below or barely within their normed expectancy intervals in the basic subjects at both early and upper elementary levels. In fact, the district, generally, was barely average relative to other districts with its same socioeconomic characteristics. (Over the several years that Los Montanas's superintendent attempted the inculcation of school effectiveness, achievement test score averages for most schools remained relatively unchanged.)

*Discussion.* Let us assume that Riverview Elementary could be a more renewing place for teachers to teach in and for students to learn in. Let us assume that there is ample room for school improvement and change and that evaluation as critical inquiry offers a viable way to go about it. How does Riverview come to see the need for critical inquiry in the first place? To what extent (if any) is there a need for collaborative intervention? How would this occur? Given our focus on the school as the unit of change, what (if any) sanctions and support at the district level are required? How would collaborators be initially legitimated or seen as credible by the staff? Even if staff members perceive a real need, how do they become interested in participating in critical inquiry? What are their rewards in this effort? Will there be the necessary resources available—in particular, time?

These are just some of the questions that come to mind as we think of trying out this proposal for inquiry and change in a school setting. These questions are not meant to be rhetorical. They arise out of an attempt to develop a mode of practice that remains consistent with our epistemological stance (and the principles and processes that flow from it) while at the same time taking into account the circumstances of schools and the obstacles they face in seeking to change.

The list of questions grows rapidly larger as one envisions critical inquiry actually operating in a school setting. What (if any) traits or skills are necessary for collaborators? When and to what extent is the critical inquiry process—critical theory and communicative competence, specifically—discussed in principle with the staff? What is to be the substance of critical inquiry? Must it always evolve under circumstances of total staff communication? How are individual socio-psychological differences handled in process? At what points do empirical-analytic and naturalistic approaches to data gathering become appropriate? How are these organized and conducted? How are the data synthesized into the process of critique? When are collaborators no longer needed?

We do not envision that the answers to all these questions can be neatly packaged and disseminated in workshops designed to train critical inquirers. Each situation will differ in profound ways, and experimentation will be necessary, while maintaining the requisite commitment to the proposed epistemology.

We can suggest some generic elements of a process that may help establish critical inquiry as a regular part of the school's culture. These elements include an operational process that (1) sees the school as the primary unit of change but recognizes that the school does not exist in a vacuum; (2) places school practitioners in central decision-making roles; (3) makes issues of values and beliefs of primary importance in school decisions; (4) emphasizes the usefulness of multiple sources and types of methods, information, and knowledge (broadly interpreted to cover all three faces of inquiry); and (5) provides support for outside collaborators while taking into account some of the difficulties collaborators face in establishing the kind of relationship we propose. (See Sirotnik, 1989 for elaboration.)

The field of education is indeed fertile ground for experimenting with evaluation as critical inquiry. Perhaps the most systematic set of implications for the practical application of critical inquiry comes from Paulo Freire's work in Brazil, Chile, and Guinea-Bissau, which fuses "critical consciousness" with pedagogical approaches for pre- and post-literacy and the ultimate goal of political awareness and empowerment.

Particularly useful are Freire's ideas on resolving problems with the role of collaborator and with content in the process of critical inquiry. Like Habermas's paradigm for communicative competence, Freire's (1973) concept of dialogical communication includes the reflexive properties of the ideal speech situation. Like Habermas, Freire is well aware of the utopianism inherent in the paradigm. But as he anticipates ideal interpersonal dialogue in the context of practice, he explicitly recognizes the need for democratic pedagogical leadership. Some one person (or group) must help dismantle the vicious circle of what Horkheimer (1972) has labeled "the eclipse of reason"—the suppression (and perhaps repression) of human introspection that Shor (1980, p. 47), building on Aronowitz's (1977) analysis, laments:

> The powerlessness and confusion in daily life can only be understood through critical thinking, yet most people are alienated from their own conceptual habits of mind. How come? Why don't masses of people engage in social reflections? Why isn't introspection an habitual feature of life? What prevents popular awareness of how the whole system operates, and which alternatives would best serve human needs? Why is political imagination driven from common experience?

Reversing this phenomenon requires pedagogical intervention and necessarily sets up an initial teacher-learner dichotomy. Freire realistically reconciles this imbalance of power by demanding a "self-effacing" stance by the teacher. In other words, the teacher must relinquish ritualistic and symbolic authority games and become an integral part of the activities and substance of learning. Thus the teacher is part learner and the learner is part teacher. This approach departs from the reflexive properties of the ideal speech situation yet is not incompatible with the psychotherapist-patient model used by Habermas for exploring undistorted communication. Whether it arises from the leadership of the school principal, district staff, one or more teachers, other collaborating forces (university-based educators), or all of the above, it seems clear to us that a culture of critically inquiring educators will not occur through some spontaneous utopian interaction. Leadership and vision are necessary prerequisites for beginning a critical inquiry project such as proposed here.

In translating Freire's teacher-student/student-teacher paradigm to one of collaborator-educator/educator-collaborator, the primary educative function of collaborators is to help teachers become enlightened about the philosophy of inquiry itself and about the preeminent role of unconstrained, normative critique. This point, of course, is central to Freire's (1973) pedagogy: "The prerequisite for [critical inquiry is] a form of education enabling the people to reflect on themselves, their responsibilities, and their role in the new cultural climate—indeed to reflect on their very *power* of reflection" (p. 16). Reflection upon reflection is a pervasive theme in the critical inquiry process, maintaining, as it does, the connection with the operating principles represented in our epistemological stance.

A second important feature of Freireian practice—problematization—suggests some strategies for generating crucial content and conducting the recursive activities of analysis, synthesis, and action based on that content. Problematization is the engagement of the group in reflecting critically on the totality of their experience. The resulting critical awareness empowers the group to alter their reality in fundamental ways.

In contrast, traditional problem solving fragments experience into discrete puzzles that appear to have solutions, provided that enough time, patience, and collective cleverness prevail. Further, such problem solving distances problem solvers (outside experts or the group itself) from their experience by considering these fragments in a purportedly objective and value-free process—problem definition, clarification, consideration of alternative solutions, decision making on courses of action, evaluation, revision, and recycling through these steps (see Schmuck and others, 1972). The likely failure of school improvement efforts conducted in this way becomes apparent when one realizes that these steps constitute the same generic problem-solving and technical assistance paradigms that have been used unsuccessfully by school interventionist-innovators for years. Even with the best-intentioned needs assessments—explorations of viable alternatives, participant decision making, and so on—these change-agent models are essentially asymmetrical and antidialogical in theory and practice. To paraphrase Freire (1978) slightly, technical assistance paradigms of educational change and innovation anesthetize school staffs and leave them acritical and naive.

## Summary and Conclusion

Space does not permit developing these ideas further, but readers are invited to consider our extended discussion elsewhere (Sirotnik and Oakes, 1986), wherein we follow through with a critical inquiry project using the Riverview experience introduced above. As promised, we have not construed program evaluation as a set of applied research technologies but rather as an ongoing, collaborative, value-driven project of organizational change and improvement.

At the heart of this project is moral argument, rooted in social justice, that maintains a dialectic around these generic categories of queries and activities:

- *Understanding the problem:* What are we doing now? How did it come to be that way?
- *Moral argument:* Whose interests are being served by the way things are? What is the nature of a just society? How does what we do (or not do) fit into this picture?
- *Seeking information:* What information and knowledge do we have or need to get that bears on the issues? Get it and continue the inquiry.

• *Taking action:* Is this the way we want things to be? What are we going to do about all this? Get on with it and continue the inquiry.

Anyone who has seriously attempted to situate complex problems in current and historical perspectives, to engage in rigorous and systematic discourse that is deliberately informed, to challenge critically, but constructively, values and human interests, and to consider actions in always ambiguous conditions and circumstances will recognize immediately that there is considerable room for doubt and uncertainty even though the inquiry stems from a moral commitment.

We suppose that taking a moral stand on evaluation appears at once to be both contrary to and consistent with our American way of life. As Americans, we are protective of our rights as individuals to make up our own minds as to what is true, beautiful, and just, yet as a democracy, we are ostensibly committed to a national community where the welfare of all people rises above that of special interest groups. No doubt this inherent paradox of, or fundamental tension in, democracy in America (noted over a century and a half ago by de Tocqueville) will continue to play itself out over the many years to come. (See, for example, the analyses by Bellah and others, 1985; and Sarason, 1986.) We have no illusions of ever achieving the perfectly just society, but as educators and human beings, we feel that this objective is most worth pursuing.

This is not unfamiliar territory, epistemologically or methodologically, in the landscape of American philosophy. Although it could be argued that the body of work left to us by John Dewey was not that of a critical theorist, Dewey (1929, pp. 51, 58) articulated a clear commitment to intellectual freedom and the democratic pursuit of knowledge in the interests of all people:

> Philosophy is looked at by those who dignify it as a subject which analyzes critically the premises that are uncritically assumed in the special sciences. . . . *Any one* is philosophical in the degree to which he makes a consistent effort in this direction. The result is emancipation.

Dewey (1920) notes: "All social institutions have a meaning, a purpose. That purpose is to set free and to develop the capacities of human individuals without respect to race, sex, class, or economic status" (p. 186).

Critical inquiry (or evaluation) as we have developed it here is, by its very nature, educational—it is informed, dialectical, and liberating. It is essential, therefore, that the process belong to those educators involved in evaluative efforts. They must view themselves as blending theory and practice, action and reflection, to transform their schools into more equitable and excellent places. They must always remember, in Dewey's (1929, p. 77) words, that

Education is by its nature an endless circle or spiral. It is an activity which includes science within itself. In its very process it sets more problems to be further studied, which then react into the educative process to change it still further, and thus demand more thought, more science, and so on, in everlasting sequence.

We would add, of course, that the science Dewey refers to be a critical one.

## References

Ackerman, B. A. *Social Justice in the Liberal State*. New Haven, Conn.: Yale University Press, 1980.

Alston, W. P. "Comments on Kohlberg's 'From Is to Ought.' " In T. Mischel (ed.), *Cognitive Development and Epistemology*. New York: Academic Press, 1971.

Aronowitz, S. "Mass Culture and the Eclipse of Reason: The Implications for Pedagogy." *College English*, 1977, *38*, 768–774.

Barker, R. G., and Gump, P. V. *Big School, Small School*. Stanford, Calif.: Stanford University Press, 1964.

Bellah, R. N., Madsen, R., Sullivan, W., Swidler, A., and Tipton, S. *Habits of the Heart: Individualism and Commitment in American Life*. New York: Harper & Row, 1985.

Berlak, A., and Berlak, H. *Dilemmas of Schooling: Teaching and Social Change*. London: Methuen, 1981.

Bernstein, R. *The Restructuring of Social and Political Theory*. Philadelphia: University of Pennsylvania Press, 1978.

Blumer, H. *Symbolic Interactionism: Perspective and Method*. Englewood Cliffs, N.J.: Prentice-Hall, 1969.

Bryk, A. S. (ed.). *Stakeholder-Based Evaluation*. New Directions for Program Evaluation, no. 17. San Francisco: Jossey-Bass, 1983.

Carr, W., and Kemmis, S. *Becoming Critical: Education, Knowledge and Action Research*. London: Falmer Press, 1986.

Coomer, D. L. "A Critical Study of Educational Evaluation Theory and Practice." Unpublished doctoral dissertation, College of Education, University of Minnesota, 1981.

Dewey, J. *Reconstruction in Philosophy*. New York: Holt, Rinehart & Winston, 1920.

Dewey, J. *The Sources of the Science of Education*. New York: Liveright, 1929.

Dworkin, R. *Taking Rights Seriously*. Cambridge, Mass.: Harvard University Press, 1977.

Eisner, E. W. "On the Uses of Educational Connoisseurship and Criticism for Evaluating Classroom Life." *Teachers College Record*, 1977, *78*, 345–358.

Ericson, D. P., and Ellett, F. S. "Interpretation, Understanding, and Educational Research." *Teachers College Record*, 1982, *83*, 497–513.

Freire, P. *Education for Critical Consciousness*. New York: Continuum, 1973.

Freire, P. *Pedagogy in Process*. New York: Seabury Press, 1978.

Geuss, R. *The Idea of a Critical Theory: Habermas and the Frankfurt School*. Cambridge, England: Cambridge University Press, 1981.

Gewirth, A. *Reason and Morality*. Chicago: University of Chicago Press, 1978.

Goodlad, J. I. *The Dynamics of Educational Change.* New York: McGraw-Hill, 1975.

Goodlad, J. I. Address before the 41st annual convention of the National School Boards Association, Dallas, Texas, April 1981.

Goodlad, J. I. *A Place Called School.* New York: McGraw-Hill, 1984.

Guba, E. G., and Lincoln, Y. S. *Effective Evaluation: Improving the Usefulness of Evaluation Results Through Responsive and Naturalistic Approaches.* San Francisco: Jossey-Bass, 1981.

Habermas, J. *Knowledge and Human Interests.* (J. Shapiro, trans.) Boston: Beacon Press, 1971.

Habermas, J. *Communication and the Evolution of Society.* (T. McCarthy, trans.) Boston: Beacon Press, 1979.

Henry, J. *On Education.* New York: Random House, 1971.

Horkheimer, M. *Critical Theory.* New York: Seabury Press, 1972.

Jackson, P. W. *Life in Classrooms.* New York: Holt, Rinehart & Winston, 1968.

Kerlinger, F. N. *Foundations of Behavioral Research.* New York: Holt, Rinehart & Winston, 1986.

Kohlberg, L. "From Is to Ought: How to Commit the Naturalistic Fallacy and Get Away with It in the Study of Moral Development." In T. Mischel (ed.), *Cognitive Development and Epistemology.* New York: Academic Press, 1971.

Lortie, D. C. *Schoolteacher: A Sociological Study.* Chicago: University of Chicago Press, 1975.

McCarthy, T. *The Critical Theory of Jürgen Habermas.* Cambridge, Mass.: MIT Press, 1978.

MacDonald, J. B. "Evaluation and the Control of Education." In D. Tawney (ed.), *Curriculum Evaluation Today: Trends and Implications.* School Council Research Studies. London: Macmillan, 1976.

Oakes, J. *Keeping Track: How Schools Structure Inequality.* New Haven, Conn.: Yale University Press, 1985.

Oakes, J. "Beneath the Bottom Line: Critical Inquiry in Vocational Education." *Journal of Vocational Education,* 1986, *11,* 33–50.

Owens, T. R. "Educational Evaluation by Adversary Proceeding." In E. R. House (ed.), *School Evaluation: The Politics and Process.* Berkeley, Calif.: McCutchan, 1973.

Parlett, M., and Hamilton, D. "Evaluation as Illumination: A New Approach to the Study of Innovatory Programs." In G. V. Glass (ed.), *Evaluation Studies Review Annual.* Vol. 1. Newbury Park, Calif.: Sage, 1976.

Patton, M. Q. (ed.). *Utilization-Focused Evaluation.* Newbury Park, Calif.: Sage, 1978.

Patton, M. Q. *Qualitative Evaluation Methods.* Newbury Park, Calif.: Sage, 1980.

Phillips, D. L. *Toward a Just Social Order.* Princeton, N.J.: Princeton University Press, 1986.

Powell, A. G., Farrar, E., and Cohen, D. K. *The Shopping Mall High School: Winners and Losers in the Educational Marketplace.* Boston: Houghton Mifflin, 1985.

Provus, M. M. *Discrepancy Evaluation.* Berkeley, Calif.: McCutchan, 1971.

Rawls, J. *A Theory of Justice.* Cambridge, Mass.: Belknap Press, 1971.

Rawls, J. "Justice as Fairness: Political Not Metaphysical." *Philosophy and Public Affairs,* 1985, *14* (3), 223–251.

Reason, P., and Rowan, J. *Human Inquiry: A Sourcebook of New Paradigm Research.* New York: Wiley, 1981.

Ricoeur, P. *Hermeneutics and the Human Sciences.* (J. B. Thompson, trans.) Cambridge, England: Cambridge University Press, 1981.

Rippey, R. M. *Studies in Transactional Evaluation*. Berkeley, Calif.: McCutchan, 1973.

Rist, R. C. "On the Relations Among Educational Research Paradigms: From Disdain to Detente." *Anthropology and Education Quarterly*, 1977, *8* (2).

Sarason, S. B. *The Culture of the School and the Problem of Change*. (Rev. ed.) Newton, Mass.: Allyn & Bacon, 1982.

Sarason, S. B. "And What Is the Public Interest?" *American Psychologist*, 1986, *41*, 899–905.

Schmuck, R. A., Runkel, P. J., Saturen, S. L., Martell, R. T., and Derr, C. B. *Handbook of Organization Development in Schools*. Palo Alto, Calif.: National Press Books, 1972.

Scriven, M. "Objectivity and Subjectivity in Educational Research." In L. G. Thomas (ed.), *Philosophical Redirection of Educational Research*, 71st Yearbook, National Society for the Study of Education. Chicago: University of Chicago Press, 1972a.

Scriven, M. "Pros and Cons About Goal-Free Evaluation." *Evaluation Comment*, 1972b, *3* (4), 1–7.

Shor, I. *Critical Teaching and Everyday Life*. Boston: South End Press, 1980.

Silberman, C. E. *Crisis in the Classroom: The Remaking of American Education*, New York: Random House, 1970.

Sirotnik, K. A. "What You See Is What You Get: Consistency, Persistency, and Mediocrity in Classrooms." *Harvard Educational Review*, 1983, *53*, 16–31.

Sirotnik, K. A. "The School as the Center of Change." In T. J. Sergiovanni and J. H. Moore (eds.), *Schooling for Tomorrow: Directing Reforms to Issues That Count*. Newton, Mass.: Allyn & Bacon, 1989.

Sirotnik, K. A., and Oakes, J. *Critical Inquiry and School Renewal: A Liberation of Method Within a Critical Theoretical Perspective*. Occasional paper no. 4, Laboratory in School and Community Education, University of California, Los Angeles, 1983.

Sirotnik, K. A., and Oakes, J. "Critical Inquiry for School Renewal: Liberating Theory and Practice." In K. A. Sirotnik and J. Oakes (eds.), *Critical Perspectives on the Organization and Improvement of Schooling*. Boston: Kluwer-Nijhoff, 1986.

Sizer, T. R. *Horace's Compromise: The Dilemma of the American High School*. Boston: Houghton Mifflin, 1984.

Spindler, G. D. (ed.). *Anthropology and Education*. Stanford, Calif.: Stanford University Press, 1955.

Stake, R. E. *Evaluating the Arts in Education: A Responsive Approach*. Columbus, Ohio: Merrill, 1975.

Stufflebeam, D. L., Foley, W. J., Gephart, W. J., Guba, E. G., Hammond, R. L., Merriman, H. O., and Provus, M. M. *Educational Evaluation and Decision Making*. Itasca, Ill.: Peacock, 1971.

Suchman, E. A. *Evaluative Research: Principles and Practice in Public Service and Social Action Programs*. New York: Russell Sage Foundation, 1967.

Taylor, C. "Interpretation and the Sciences of Man." In F. R. Dallmayr and T. A. McCarthy (eds.), *Understanding and Social Inquiry*. Notre Dame, Ind.: University of Notre Dame, 1977.

Thompson, M. S. *Benefit-Cost Analysis for Program Evaluation*. Newbury Park, Calif.: Sage, 1980.

Van Manen, M.J.M. "An Exploration of Alternative Research Orientations in Social Education." *Theory and Research in Social Education*, 1975, *3*, 1–28.

Waller, W. *The Sociology of Teaching*. New York: Wiley, 1932.

Williams, D. D. (ed.). *Naturalistic Evaluation*. New Directions for Program Evaluation, no. 30. San Francisco: Jossey-Bass, 1986.

Wolcott, H. F. *The Man in the Principal's Office: An Ethnography*. New York: Holt, Rinehart & Winston, 1973.

*Kenneth A. Sirotnik is professor and chair, Policy, Governance, and Administration, College of Education, University of Washington. His work and publications range widely over many topics, including measurement, statistics, evaluation, computer technology, educational policy, organizational change, and school improvement.*

*Jeannie Oakes is associate professor in the Graduate School of Education, University of California, Los Angeles, and consultant for the RAND Corporation. Her work focuses on organizational structures and administrative practices and their consequences for the schooling opportunities for minority and disadvantaged students.*

*Because at-risk status is socially constructed, school-level programs designed for at-risk students and their evaluations should explicitly address the theoretical underpinnings of at-riskness as enacted within the particular school culture. One way of doing this is through critical inquiry.*

# At-Risk Programs:
# Evaluation and Critical Inquiry

*Virginia Richardson*

This volume is concerned with the reconceptualization of the theory and practice of educational evaluation such that a program evaluation (1) is designed in relationship to and provides an understanding of the broader social, political, and economic context in which the program operates; and (2) explicitly embraces the normative stance of social justice. Sirotnik and Oakes (this volume) propose the corollary that such evaluations would be designed to be ameliorative; that is, they should be integral and essential elements of school change and reform processes. This chapter is meant to provide an example of how such thinking, methodology, and practice would develop around a type of program that is being advocated today—one designed for at-risk students.

Because of the complexity of the task of reconceptualizing the evaluation process toward a process that contains an explicit normative social goal and is designed for purposes of fundamental change, the arguments in this chapter will not be straightforward. I will first discuss the normative stance I wish to take and the conflict between educational activities designed to meet this norm and those that function to maintain the status quo. I then suggest that a critical inquiry approach requires the evaluator to examine the assumptions and theoretical frameworks that undergird a particular program. The importance of this examination is illustrated by suggesting two very different ways that programs for at-

I wish to thank Gary Fenstermacher for suggesting that I begin my thinking on the topic of normative stance with the caring ethic rather than notions of social justice and Ken Sirotnik for suggesting the relationship between them.

risk students could evolve, depending on different theories of how students become at-risk. The first theory is based on a predictive, or actuarial, model of the at-risk process. The second suggests that the definition of at-riskness is socially constructed.

Programs based on both theories could work to maintain the status quo; however, with the addition of the type of critical inquiry discussed by Sirotnik and Oakes (this volume), programs that acknowledge the second theory could lead to fundamental change. Using examples from a recently conducted ethnographic study of twelve at-risk students in grades 2 and 3 (Richardson, Casanova, Placier, and Guilfoyle, 1989), I will indicate how these different approaches affected which children were identified as at-risk and what happened to them within the schooling contexts. Using this material as a base, I will then conclude that the only way that ameliorative evaluation may be carried out is within a school and with (not on) the personnel who are closest to the students. This conclusion is similar to Fenstermacher and Amarel's (1983) thesis that those closest to the students are in the best position to make decisions concerning educational practices: "The more distal authorities intervene to regulate the processes and procedures of school practice, the greater the risk to humanity's interests" (p. 403).

## The Normative Stance

Ericson (this volume) points out that there are a number of different approaches to the concept of social justice and that the issues are quite complex. Rather than grapple with these issues in laying out my normative stance, I would prefer to select one that brings the goals somewhat closer to the daily lives of teachers and students. Using Noddings (1984) work on the ethics of caring, the normative framework advanced here is that a top priority for any educational program is that students are cared for; programs should be developed that do not harm and that nurture and help all children grow intellectually, socially, and emotionally. This norm is not, of course, at odds with that of social justice; in fact, one could think of the social justice goal that all children receive equal access to educational opportunities as being enacted through the caring ethic. However, as Noddings (1984) points out, actions framed within a caring ethic do not depend "wholly on rules—not upon a prior determination of what is fair and equitable" (p. 13) but on the situations and other conditions as viewed by both caregiver and cared-for as they negotiate together their relationship and their context. This norm, then, seems closer to what it is we want for our children as they make their way through school.

While the norm of caring may seem an obvious one for schooling, one that is aspired to by everyone, we only have to examine a common aspect of American education to see how a competing goal creates educational activities that violate the caring norm. Consider, for example, the practice of giving grades. Whereas high grades may operate as an incentive, low grades are hurtful. There is nothing in the literature that convinces me that low grades act as an incentive for most students who receive them, particularly elementary school students; there is much in the theoretical and empirical literature to suggest that in the long run, low grades may be detrimental to student learning. Crooks (1988), for example, concluded a literature review of classroom evaluation practices by suggesting that "too much emphasis has been placed on the grading function of evaluation, and too little on its role in assisting students to learn" (p. 668). He based this conclusion on evidence that, for most students, normative grading produces negative consequences. One of these outcomes was described in a recently published case study of an urban high school by Farrell, Peguero, Lindsey, and White (1988) who suggested that the stress of constantly being faced with expectations that cannot be met may lead to a passive, self-defeating view of school as boring and to subsequent dropping out of school. The research on retention, an outcome of failing grades, indicates negative effects (Shepard and Smith, 1989).

Further, grading makes it difficult for teachers to care for their students. This may, in fact, be why teachers, particularly elementary teachers, are so uncomfortable with the grading process. In extensive teacher belief interviews conducted by Richardson, Casanova, Placier, and Guilfoyle (1989), grading was seen by most teachers as one of the most difficult elements of their role. In a current study of the teaching of reading comprehension (Anders and Richardson, 1988), teacher belief interviews reflect the same concerns, and the most time-consuming topic discussed in the critical inquiry staff development program concerned teachers' anxieties about grading and assessment. Giving low grades and utilizing standardized tests are antithetical to sound pedagogical principles that suggest that students should be provided with success experiences.

Grading in its present form, particularly that employing the notion of the grading curve, is used for purposes other than caring for the intellectual, social, and emotional growth of children. These purposes appear to be related more to the hidden functions of schooling discussed by Sirotnik and Oakes (this volume), which include screening students out of the system (through flunking or dropping out of school) or to lower-tracked curricula (Oakes, 1985). The strong relationship between students dropping out and such factors as socioeconomic and minority status suggests that grading also functions to maintain the status quo.

It may be the case that individuals who advocate programs that serve these hidden functions do so in the belief that the programs will, in fact, care for children in need. The problems may be conceptualized and programs developed to respond to social problems, but such programs may also respond to the socially defined "realities" of schooling, such as the requirements for accountability. These "realities" end up shaping programs so that they function to maintain the status quo. For example, the need for ensuring that federal funds are spent on students who truly require such support leads to the development of easily applied indicators of needy children. This policy labels children as deficient on the basis of characteristics over which they have no control. Labeling is often educationally harmful to children (see, for example, Schell, 1975). The indicators developed to meet requirements for accountability either ensure that low-income, ethnically and linguistically different children are labeled, as they are in various at-risk programs being developed, or function to do so, as in the case of Special Education and Learning Disabilities programs (see, for example, Sigmon, 1987; Coles, 1987). Thus the strong concerns for children, tempered by political, social, and bureaucratic realities, may lead to a way of defining the problem and developing a program that results in the antithesis of the initial social goal.

Nowhere is this as evident as in the identification of and educational programs for "special" populations of children, such as those at-risk. The next section describes two theories of the identification of at-risk students and the role of schools in helping these students. This section is followed by a short summary of the relevant results of a study that found differences in approaches of two schools that subscribed to different philosophies related to educating at-risk students and the effects of these differences on students identified as such. The last section describes how an approach to evaluation—critical inquiry—could affect how teachers think about the problem of at-risk students, the numbers and types of students identified as at-risk, and the educational program for those students.

## The Identification of At-Risk Students and the Responsibility of the School

While the concept of at-risk, when applied to an individual, has been used in medical and psychiatric literature for some time (see Garmezy, 1974; Werner, Bierman, and French, 1971), this concept has only recently been used in educational literature and policy discussions. For example, the term *high risk students* has been in use as an ERIC descriptor only since 1982. *At-risk* is a term that focuses attention on children who have the potential for failing in school; dropping out; committing suicide; becoming delinquent, drug or alcohol dependent, or pregnant; or falling into other adverse states (Brown, 1986). In schooling discussions, the term *at-risk* refers primarily to those students who are or have the potential for failing or dropping out, or both. The term also encompasses such descriptors as disadvantaged, low SES, underachieving, problem children—terms that describe populations of students for whom the schools traditionally have been less than successful. Two models can be used to explain the current interest in at-risk students.

*The Epidemiological Model.* In educational discourse today, the term *at-risk* has a medical or epidemiological connotation. In the epidemiological model, an at-risk student has certain inherent characteristics that may lead to some adverse state (or disease) unless something intervenes. The "diseases" in education are dropping out, failure, teenage suicide, and so on. Certain characteristics may relate to the acquisition or manifestation of the diseases, including poverty, single-parent homes, or personal characteristics such as ethnic or linguistic diversity (see, for example, studies by Broman, Bien, and Shaughnessy, 1985, and by Spivack, Marcuso, and Swift, 1986). While certain types of classroom behavior, such as low attendance and failing grades, may also be used as indicators, the causes of such behaviors are assumed to relate to particular background and personal characteristics.

In this view, the educational system intervenes to break the relationship between background characteristics and eventual adverse outcomes. The federally funded Head Start and Follow Through programs were based on such a model. (See Baratz and Baratz, 1982, for a critique of such programs.) Children from low SES families were eligible for programs designed to alleviate at-risk factors assumed to be generated in the home environment. This assumption was based on the empirically demonstrated relationship between economic status of the family and achievement in school.

The decision to employ such a model meets the needs of national policymakers, who require an easily identifiable group of students for purposes of categorical funding. Unfortunately, however, this model assumes that the problem is inherent in the student, and the search for cause is limited to the characteristics of the students themselves. Characteristics of society and schools are left unexamined (Wehlage and Rutter, 1986). This leads to the labeling of students as inherently deficient and to the assumption that the role of the schools as institutions is to fix the student. Further, the model does not explain why some students with similar predisposing characteristics as those who are failing may succeed in school or why a child could be at-risk at one point in time and not at another or at-risk in one school and not in another. We must look to a model where the focus is not just on students as deficient but on the interaction between the student and the schooling context.

*The Social Constructivist Model.* This model takes an interactive view of the identification of at-risk students in which the perception of at-riskness is constructed within a particular social or cultural context. As Nelkin (1985) suggests, "It is the social system, the world view, the ideological premises of a group or a society that shapes perceptions of risk" (p. 16). Thus the person considered at-risk, the reasons for this consideration, and the ways in which the school responds are constructed in the context of the school and classroom.

This model suggests that the child brings to the classroom a certain number of characteristics that have been shaped by background and past experiences in school. What happens in the classroom is affected, in part, by school factors, which are often influenced by the school district, the state, and so on. The child interacts with a classroom context that includes other children, teachers, and materials. Mehan, Hertweck, and Meihls (1986), in a study of the special education referral process, suggest that the perceptions of a student's classroom performance is a function of the norms, expectations, and values of the perceiver interacting with the essential nature of the student (see also Erickson, 1985; Page, 1987; Smith, 1983). Mehan and colleagues (1986) conclude, "The teacher's decision to refer students is only partially grounded in the students' behavior. It is grounded also in the categories that the teacher brings to the interaction, including the expectations for academic performance and norms for appropriate classroom conduct" (p. 87). The focus of this approach, then, is not on the child alone but on the interaction between the child and the nested contexts of classroom, school, school district, and state.

## At-Risk in Practice

In a recent ethnographic study of twelve elementary students identified as at-risk by their teachers in two schools that were located in two school districts, my colleagues and I found that the social constructivist model more closely explained how at-risk children were identified and dealt with in the schools (Richardson, Casanova, Placier, and Guilfoyle, 1989). Teachers exhibited a fluid notion of the concept of at-risk. At the beginning of the year, they identified students at-risk in their classrooms as those who were not fitting in socially, were performing poorly on tests, or were not working as they should. At the end, students still considered at-risk were those who had not responded adequately to the attempts teachers made to help them adjust. While the numbers of students identified as at-risk by a particular teacher remained constant from the beginning to the end of the year, the names of students did not. Further, in two team teaching situations there was only an approximately 50 percent overlap between the list generated by the two teachers in each team. By examining the belief interviews of teachers, in addition to analyzing the classroom observations, we were able to indicate how a given teacher's expectations for academic and/or social behavior in a classroom affected whether or not a student was identified as at-risk. It was clear also that a child thought to be a problem by a teacher is indeed at-risk, in part because of the transmission of the teacher's opinion to the child as well as to the rest of the students in the classroom.

There were, however, differences between the two schools in terms of the ways in which at-riskness was viewed and dealt with. The schools both served a low-income minority student body; in one case Hispanic, in the other, black. Both had vigorous minority women principals who were thought of as effective leaders. The climate of both schools was similar: warm and caring, with all adults feeling responsible for all children. However, school A was located within a small, tightly coupled school district that was exceedingly concerned with standardized test scores and standardized instructional delivery systems. The school was seen by the district as well able to handle at-risk children because of its large number of experts: a bilingual speech and hearing specialist, bilingual and nonbilingual learning disability (LD) teachers, a bilingual reading specialist, and so on. When classroom teachers talked about their at-risk students, they used the diagnostic language of experts, focusing on the child's problems. One child, for example, was described as dyspraxic by the classroom teacher as well as the school psychologist. The teachers seemed constantly under stress to produce higher test scores at the same time as they questioned their validity. Teachers, students, and their parents talked a lot about failure. The school had recently developed an informal approach for dealing with the testing situation by deciding that LD students should not take their grade-level standardized reading and mathematics tests. Such a policy could drive up the number of students labeled as learning disabled. As it turned out, a greater proportion of students were identified as at-risk at school A than at school B, although the schools' populations were similar.

Life was hectic for those students identified as at-risk in school A. One third-grade student that we followed divided his time among six different classrooms in one day. Needless to say, the programs were fragmented and incoherent, and considerable time was wasted in moving from classroom to classroom. Further, he missed many of the activities in his homeroom. The complexity of the programs for at-risk students made it hard for teachers to organize sustained activities for their students. Further, teachers resented "losing" their students for part of the day, feeling that they could not get to know these students as well as they should.

School B was located in a very large school district that has been described variously as decentralized or ungovernable. School B, a small school, had no major preoccupation with at-risk students. The teachers that were interviewed, as well as the counselor and principal, expressed a philosophy that was child-centered and developmental. For the counselor, all students could be at-risk at one point or another. The important thing for her was observing the child within the context of the classroom, because the classroom could be creating the problems for the child. The school had adopted a teacher assistance team program (see Chalfant and Pysh, 1981); a team of teachers met once a week to provide other teachers with alternatives for their "problem" students. The emphasis in the school was placed on in-classroom alternatives for at-risk students. There were few experts available to the school, and pulling students out of the classroom was rare. Thus the teachers observed in the study scheduled time according to task, and their approach to the teaching-learning process was to create an environment in which students could learn at their own pace without thinking of themselves as failures and losing self-esteem. In the interviews with teachers, students, and their parents, no one mentioned the word *failure*, and little anxiety was expressed about standardized test scores.

Ironically, in the year of the study, the scores on standardized tests for the grades we studied in school A, a school that focused on at-risk students and test scores, continued to be the lowest in the area, while the scores in school B were above average for the district and nation.

In both schools we found that the social construction of at-risk status helped explain the educators' beliefs and actions toward children who did not adapt well to the social and academic context. School district policies laid an additional burden on school A in the form of a set of assumptions that matched more closely those of the predictive, child-as-problem model described above. These assumptions included the technocratic notion (see Wise, 1979) that a distal authority could decide on the best teaching approach for all schools and teachers in the district and the narrowly psychometric view that absolute and valid indicators may be developed to identify at-risk children without consideration of school context. These assumptions, in combination with the required accounting mechanisms that accompany federal and state funding of categorical programs, could lead to an ever-increasing percentage of students labeled as at-risk.

There were, however, a number of common aspects to the approach to at-riskness across the two schools. The teachers were aware, in part, of the situation-specific nature of the identification of at-risk students. The teachers all stated that students who were at-risk in one classroom would not necessarily be considered at-risk in another. This finding was similar to that of Erickson (1985), who concluded that teachers, because they consider what one student is doing in relation to what others are doing, are "intuitive social constructivists" (p. 7). The teachers were generally unwilling to attribute a student's lack of success to the student or to their own instructional programs. They instead looked outside the classroom to find the cause of students' problems. These causes most often resided in their students' home lives and parents. Their frustration with the parents of at-risk students was palpable, and the assumption that the not-at-risk students came from strong families was universal. While some of the teachers' concerns about particular parents were well founded, other concerns were not. Although the teachers did not seem to develop negative expectations for individual students on the basis of their difficult family backgrounds, they did build negative images of families on the basis of the students' problem behavior in class.

What was not seen by the teachers was their own role in the creation of an environment and set of expectations that affected their labeling of at-risk students as well as the students' behavior—that the concept of "unsuccessful" or "at-riskness" was defined by themselves and differed from teacher to teacher. The teachers saw, in part, the effect of the context on the behavior of their students, and they understood that a child may not be considered at-risk in another context. But they seemed unaware of the way in which they affected that context through their beliefs and understandings about students, learning, and teaching. Although their strong sense of efficacy and feelings of responsibility for their students helped the teachers create a powerful and unique learning environment in their classrooms that was beneficial for most of their students, this attitude also made it difficult for them to understand and question the effects of this environment on students who did not adapt well to it.

This study suggests that the notions of at-risk, problem students, low achievement, and so on are socially constructed within classrooms and schools. The process is, of course, affected by school district, state, and federal conceptions and deliberations. This interactive view of the identification of at-risk students requires an evaluation model that is compatible with the inherent assumptions, as discussed in the following section.

## The Evaluation of At-Risk Programs

A typical positivist evaluation of programs for at-risk students could begin with the development of an operational definition of at-risk status or the acceptance of one used in the particular program. This definition would allow for objective, absolute measures or indicators that could be used to identify the sample of students under consideration and to follow their progress. This identification would be accomplished regardless of the varying contexts or cultures of the schools in which the programs were operating. Thus, for example, grades or scores on standardized tests could be used as indicators of at-risk status or as pre- and post measures, even though a partial cause of initial low scores may rest with the school in which an at-risk program is operating. The evaluators could then look for changes in these indicators of at-risk status that could be attributed to the at-risk program. However, pretest data are not really "pre," because such indicators and the program to be evaluated are embedded in an ongoing school culture. Failing to examine the interactions among the school culture, the particular program features, and student learning results in findings that are neither useful for the specific program nor generalizable to other contexts.

As others have pointed out in this volume, it is also important to examine the broad social and theoretical frameworks that undergird a program. For example, an evaluation of the at-risk program in school A should critically examine the fundamental assumptions of the predictive framework that identifies the child as a problem. Without such a critical examination, an evaluation may conclude that not enough was being done for at-risk students. Using objective, absolute measures of at-risk, the evaluators may find that more students should be labeled as being at-risk or that the wrong students were "treated." The evaluation might develop several other categories of at-risk students and suggest that they receive differentiated instructional programs. A process evaluation may conclude that time on task for these students was low and therefore suggest that the process of moving from teacher to teacher should be faster. From a more critical analysis, these possible conclusions are trivial at best and at worst the implementation of these suggestions could harm children. Thus the narrow, psychometric framework that is so much an integral element of positivist evaluations may contribute to the maintenance of the status quo.

This analysis suggests, then, that the assumptions inherent in the widely accepted positivist evaluation paradigm are more closely aligned to the epidemiological theory of at-risk status than to the social constructivist model. And yet, as pointed out above, the social constructivist theory was able to account for observed educational practice in terms of the beliefs of those educators closest to the students and their actions toward them.

Let us now consider the nature of a program that would be framed within the social constructivist theory and such a program's evaluation system. Since the school is essential in the formation of the expectations for students and the definition of at-risk status, the program would focus at the school level, and all personnel would be involved. Depending on the level of the school, students would also be involved, since they contribute to the school culture. A major aspect of the at-risk program would involve all teachers, specialists, and administrators in a process of reflection on and analysis of the school environment and the nature of the student population. As mentioned above, in the Richardson and colleagues (1989) study, the teachers did not express an understanding of the ways in which their own classrooms affected the behavior and thus the identification of the at-risk students. Thus a major element in the program would allow and provide support for teachers to reflect on their beliefs and expectations about students and learning, study cases of students, classrooms and schools (Carter and Richardson, 1989), and talk with those who understand the culture of their students. Other aspects of a school-based program for at-risk students could involve school-level efforts to communicate with parents and work with social agencies, the institution of a process that provides immediate help for teachers who are having problems with individual students, and the introduction of a child-centered, developmental approach toward children. Other program features for at-risk students have been suggested elsewhere (Heckman, Wilson, and Fenstermacher, 1988).

The evaluation component of such a program would take the form of critical inquiry. Critical inquiry in a school reform process may, in fact, become an element of the change process. Particular forms of data gathering may go well beyond being of heuristic value. For example, the very gathering of data on the beliefs of the participants could change the nature of their beliefs and, perhaps, their practices. While in positivist evaluation this could cause validity problems, such is not the case with critical inquiry.

The goal-setting process for the school would in itself be a lengthy process, during which the kinds of theories expressed above would be thoroughly examined. Again, this examination would begin to change understandings and practices. The following goals are not suggested for prescriptive purposes but to indicate how the goal-setting process and baseline data collection in a school reform process could in themselves change the operation and culture of a school. The goals for a school undergoing reform in defining and aiding at-risk students could be the following:

• To reduce the numbers of context-specific at-risk students—that is, students who would be viewed as at-risk or problems in one context and not another (Richardson, Casanova, Placier, and Guilfoyle, 1989)

• To create a school and classroom environment and structure in which all students, including those who need extra help, are able to view themselves as good students

• To join with parents, the community, and social services to help all students grow intellectually, socially, and emotionally.

The type of data that would be useful in tracking students throughout the process of reform could include:

• Baseline data concerning the numbers and names of students who have been labeled and the circumstances under which the labeling occurred; observational data on the students within their present classroom; and interview data from the students, their parents, their teachers, and themselves on how they view their present circumstances and performance within it

- Data on teachers', specialists', and administrators' beliefs toward teaching and learning and at-risk students, school environment, and barriers to effective teaching
- A thorough analysis of the educational programs received by each student labeled as at-risk, including an analysis of the enacted curriculum (Doyle, forthcoming) in each classroom across a school day, week, and semester.

One can see how the collection of this data could affect what happens to students. As my colleagues and I have found in conducting a similar process regarding the teaching of reading comprehension in grades 4, 5, and 6 in three schools (Anders and Richardson, 1988), the process of thinking about questions during initial belief interviews and of verbalizing the responses sometimes changed teachers' priorities, understandings, and classroom practices, as did the process of testing students in their classrooms with a new reading measure that attempts to incorporate current cognitive research on reading comprehension. This measure was developed at the Center for the Study of Reading, University of Illinois, for the State of Illinois Goal Assessment Program and includes a section designed to activate and test background knowledge and a long passage followed by a set of questions, many of which have more than one "correct" answer. After the measure was given to all students in the study, a number of teachers began to pay more attention to activating background knowledge prior to asking students to read a passage. Thus, such data is not pretest; rather, its collection is part of the reform process.

It is also clear that educators participating in the reform process must be actively involved and committed to the critical inquiry process. The examination of teacher beliefs and school culture is a risky process and requires a high level of mutual trust and commitment to the process. Because critical inquiry is an integral element of the reform process, it must be managed and controlled by the personnel within the school. Outside experts may be helpful to the process; however, their involvement should be as consultants.

The critical inquiry approach would allow the adults in a school to examine the ways in which at-riskness is socially constructed within their school and to develop and test ways of reducing the detrimental effects of labeling while at the same time improving the educational process for those who are not adapting to the school culture and demands.

## Conclusion

The arguments in this chapter suggest that many programs and practices in education function to conserve the social, political, and economic status quo by maintaining a strong relationship between socioeconomic status and educational attainment. The needs of many students, particularly low SES and ethnically and linguistically different students, are not well met by the educational system. If the normative goal implied in notions of social justice is to redress these problems and meet the needs of all students, programs designed to do so must be examined in a critical manner. The study by Richardson and colleagues (1989) suggests that many programs designed for at-risk students are based on a theoretical framework that functions to maintain the status quo by labeling certain students as deficient on the basis of characteristics over which students have no control. The social constructivist framework not only more adequately explains what happens in practice but also is more useful for thinking about fundamental change. This change of approach would lead to schools in which teachers are able to care for all students, which in turn would meet the equity norms embedded in notions of social justice.

An evaluation of such a program could not be based on assumptions inherent in a positivist evaluation model. Critical inquiry, which supplies evaluation with a normative base, is more suitable to a process that could lead to fundamental change in schools. This process would become an essential element of reform—one that acknowledges and therefore plans for the effects of data gathering on the change process and one that examines the broader social, political, and economic frameworks as well as the beliefs and expectations of the educators who are responsible for caring for students.

In a recent treatise on schooling, Hamilton (1989) concluded that schooling is "simultaneously a site of social regulation and a site of social redefinition" (p. 154). Recently, various actions by local, state, and federal officials have emphasized the first function—that of social regulation. The process of critical inquiry may redress this imbalance and push schools toward the function of social redefinition.

### References

Anders, P., and Richardson, V. "A Study of Teachers' Research-Based Instruction of Reading Comprehension." Paper presented at the annual meeting of the American Educational Research Association, New Orleans, La., 1988.

Baratz, J., and Baratz, S. C. "Early Childhood Intervention: The Social Base of Institutional Racism." In Yetman, N. R. (ed.), *Majority and Minority: The Dynamics of Race and Ethnicity in American Life.* (3rd ed.) Newton, Mass.: Allyn & Bacon, 1982.

Broman, S., Bien, E., and Shaughnessy, P. *Low Achieving Children: The First Seven Years.* Hillsdale, N.J.: Erlbaum, 1985.

Brown, R. "State Responsibility for At-Risk Youth." *Metropolitan Education,* 1986, 2, 5–12.

Carter, K., and Richardson, V. "The Content of the Initial Year of Teaching Programs." *Elementary School Journal,* 1989, 89, 405–420.

Chalfant, J., and Pysh, M. V. "Teacher Assistance Teams: A Model for Within-Building Problem Solving." In Council for Exceptional Children, *Counterpoint*, 1981.

Coles, G. *The Learning Mystique: A Critical Look at "Learning Disabilities"*. New York: Pantheon, 1987.

Crooks, T. "Classroom Evaluation Practices." *Review of Educational Research*, 1988, *58* (4), 438–481.

Doyle, W. "The Curriculum of Teacher Education." *Educational Researcher*, forthcoming.

Erickson, F. "Toward a Theory of Student Status as Socially Constructed." Paper presented at the annual meeting of the American Educational Research Association, Chicago, Ill., April 1985.

Farrell, E., Peguero, G., Lindsey, R., and White, R. "Giving Voice to High School Students: Pressure and Boredom, Ya Know What I'm Sayin'?" *AERJ*, 1988, *25*, 489–502.

Fenstermacher, G., and Amarel, M. "The Interests of the Student, the State and Humanity in Education." In L. Shulman and G. Sykes (eds.), *Handbook of Teaching and Policy*. New York: Longman, 1983.

Garmezy, N. "The Study of Competence in Children At-Risk for Severe Psychopathology." In M. C. Wittrock (ed.), *Review of Research in Education*. Itasca, Ill.: Peacock, 1974.

Hamilton, D. *Towards a Theory of Schooling*. London: Falmer Press, 1989.

Heckman, P., Wilson, C., and Fenstermacher, G. *Positioning Students for Success*. Tucson, Ariz.: College of Education, University of Arizona, 1988.

Mehan, H., Hertweck, A., and Meihls, J. L. *Handicapping the Handicapped*. Stanford, Calif.: Stanford University Press, 1986.

Nelkin, D. "Introduction: Analyzing Risk." In D. Nelkin (ed.), *The Language of Risk*. Newbury Park, Calif.: Sage, 1985.

Noddings, N. *Caring: A Feminist Approach to Ethics and Moral Education*. Berkeley: University of California Press, 1984.

Oakes, J. *Keeping Track: How Schools Structure Inequality*. New Haven, Conn.: Yale University Press, 1985.

Richardson, V., Casanova, U., Placier, P., and Guilfoyle, K. *School Children At-Risk in School*. London: Falmer Press, 1989.

Schell, T. J. *Labelling Madness*. Englewood Cliffs, N.J.: Prentice-Hall, 1975.

Sigmon, S. B. *Radical Analysis of Special Education: Focus on Historical Development and Learning Disabilities*. London: Falmer Press, 1987.

Spivack, G., Marcuso, J., and Swift, M. "Early Classroom Behavior and Later Misconduct." *Developmental Psychology*, 1986, *22*, 124–131.

Wehlage, G. G., and Rutter, R. A. "Dropping Out: How Much Do Schools Contribute to the Problem?" *Teachers College Record*, 1986, *87*, 364–392.

Werner, E., Bierman, J., and French, F. *The Children of Kauai: A Longitudinal Study from the Prenatal Period Through Age 10*. Honolulu: University of Hawaii Press, 1971.

Wise, A. E. *Legislated Learning*. Berkeley, Calif.: University of California Press, 1979.

*Virginia Richardson is professor of teaching and teacher education in the College of Education, University of Arizona. Her research interests include teachers' beliefs and practices, teacher change, teacher education, and school culture. She also writes on the relationship among educational practice, policy, and research and on qualitative methodology.*

# INDEX

# ORDERING INFORMATION

NEW DIRECTIONS FOR PROGRAM EVALUATION is a series of paperback books that presents the latest techniques and procedures for conducting useful evaluation studies of all types of programs. Books in the series are published quarterly, in Fall, Winter, Spring, and Summer, and are available for purchase by subscription as well as by single copy.

SUBSCRIPTIONS for 1990 cost $48.00 for individuals (a savings of 20 percent over single-copy prices) and $64.00 for institutions, agencies, and libraries. Please do not send institutional checks for personal subscriptions. Standing orders are accepted.

SINGLE COPIES cost $14.95 when payment accompanies order. (California, New Jersey, New York, and Washington, D.C., residents please include appropriate sales tax.) Billed orders will be charged postage and handling.

DISCOUNTS FOR QUANTITY ORDERS are available. Please write to the address below for information.

ALL ORDERS must include either the name of an individual or an official purchase order number. Please submit your order as follows:
  *Subscriptions:* specify series and year subscription is to begin
  *Single copies:* include individual title code (such as PE1)

MAIL ALL ORDERS TO:
  Jossey-Bass Inc., Publishers
  350 Sansome Street
  San Francisco, California 94104